THE MIGHTY·NEIN ORIGINS™

YASHA NYDOORIN

CRITICAL ROLE

• Y. N. •

THE MIGHTY NEIN ORIGINS

CRITICAL ROLE
THE MIGHTY·NEIN
ORIGINS™

YASHA NYDOORIN

WRITTEN BY

Cecil Castellucci

WITH

| Ashley Johnson | *AND* | Matthew Mercer |

OF
CRITICAL ROLE

ART BY

William Kirkby

COLORS BY

Diana Sousa

COLOR ASSISTANCE BY

Paulo Crocomo

LETTERS BY

Ariana Maher

DARK HORSE BOOKS

PRESIDENT AND PUBLISHER
Mike Richardson

EDITOR
Rachel Roberts

ASSOCIATE EDITOR
Jenny Blenk

ASSISTANT EDITOR
Anastacia Ferry

DESIGNER
Cindy Cacerez-Sprague

DIGITAL ART TECHNICIAN
Samantha Hummer

EXECUTIVE VICE PRESIDENT Neil Hankerson CHIEF FINANCIAL OFFICER Tom Weddle CHIEF INFORMATION OFFICER Dale LaFountain VICE PRESIDENT OF LICENSING Tim Wiesch VICE PRESIDENT OF MARKETING Matt Parkinson VICE PRESIDENT OF PRODUCTION AND SCHEDULING Vanessa Todd-Holmes VICE PRESIDENT OF BOOK TRADE AND DIGITAL SALES Mark Bernardi VICE PRESIDENT OF PRODUCT DEVELOPMENT Randy Lahrman GENERAL COUNSEL Ken Lizzi EDITOR IN CHIEF Dave Marshall EDITORIAL DIRECTOR Davey Estrada SENIOR BOOKS EDITOR Chris Warner DIRECTOR OF SPECIALTY PROJECTS Cary Grazzini ART DIRECTOR Lia Ribacchi DIRECTOR OF DIGITAL ART AND PREPRESS Matt Dryer SENIOR DIRECTOR OF LICENSED PUBLICATIONS Michael Gombos DIRECTOR OF CUSTOM PROGRAMS Kari Yadro DIRECTOR OF INTERNATIONAL LICENSING Kari Torson

Published by Dark Horse Books, a division of Dark Horse Comics LLC
10956 SE Main Street, Milwaukie, OR 97222

DarkHorse.com ◆ Comic Shop Locator Service: ComicShopLocator.com ◆ CritRole.com

First edition: July 2022
Ebook ISBN: 978-1-50672-389-1
Hardcover ISBN: 978-1-50672-379-2

1 3 5 7 9 10 8 6 4 2
Printed in China

Library of Congress Cataloging-in-Publication Data

Names: Castellucci, Cecil, 1969- writer. | Mercer, Matthew, 1982- writer. | Johnson, Ashley, writer. | Kirkby, William T., artist. | Sousa, Diana, colourist. | Maher, Ariana, letterer.
Title: Critical role : the Mighty Nein origins, Yasha Nydoorin / written by Cecil Castellucci ; with Matthew Mercer and Ashley Johnson of Critical Role ; art by William Kirkby ; colors by Diana Sousa ; letters by Ariana Maher.
Other titles: Critical Role (Game)
Description: First edition. | Milwaukie, OR : Dark Horse Books, 2021. | Summary: "For Yasha, there has always been a storm on the horizon. Maybe it formed with her adoption by the Dolorov people in the harsh lands of Xhorhas. Or perhaps when she fell for her first love, Zuala. Or still later, when grief and madness drove her from her village and out into--somewhere else. Maybe, on the other hand, Yasha IS the storm. Celebrated writer Cecil Castellucci joins artist William Kirkby, colorist Diana Sousa, and letterer Ariana Maher, with Matthew Mercer and Ashley Johnson of Critical Role, to draw back the curtain on the tumultuous past of the Mighty Nein's Yasha Nydoorin"-- Provided by publisher.
Identifiers: LCCN 2021010421 (print) | LCCN 2021010422 (ebook) | ISBN 9781506723792 (hardcover) | ISBN 9781506723891 (ebook)
Subjects: LCSH: Comic books, strips, etc.
Classification: LCC PN6728.C6996 C37 2021 (print) | LCC PN6728.C6996 (ebook) | DDC 741.5/973--dc23
LC record available at https://lccn.loc.gov/2021010421
LC ebook record available at https://lccn.loc.gov/2021010422

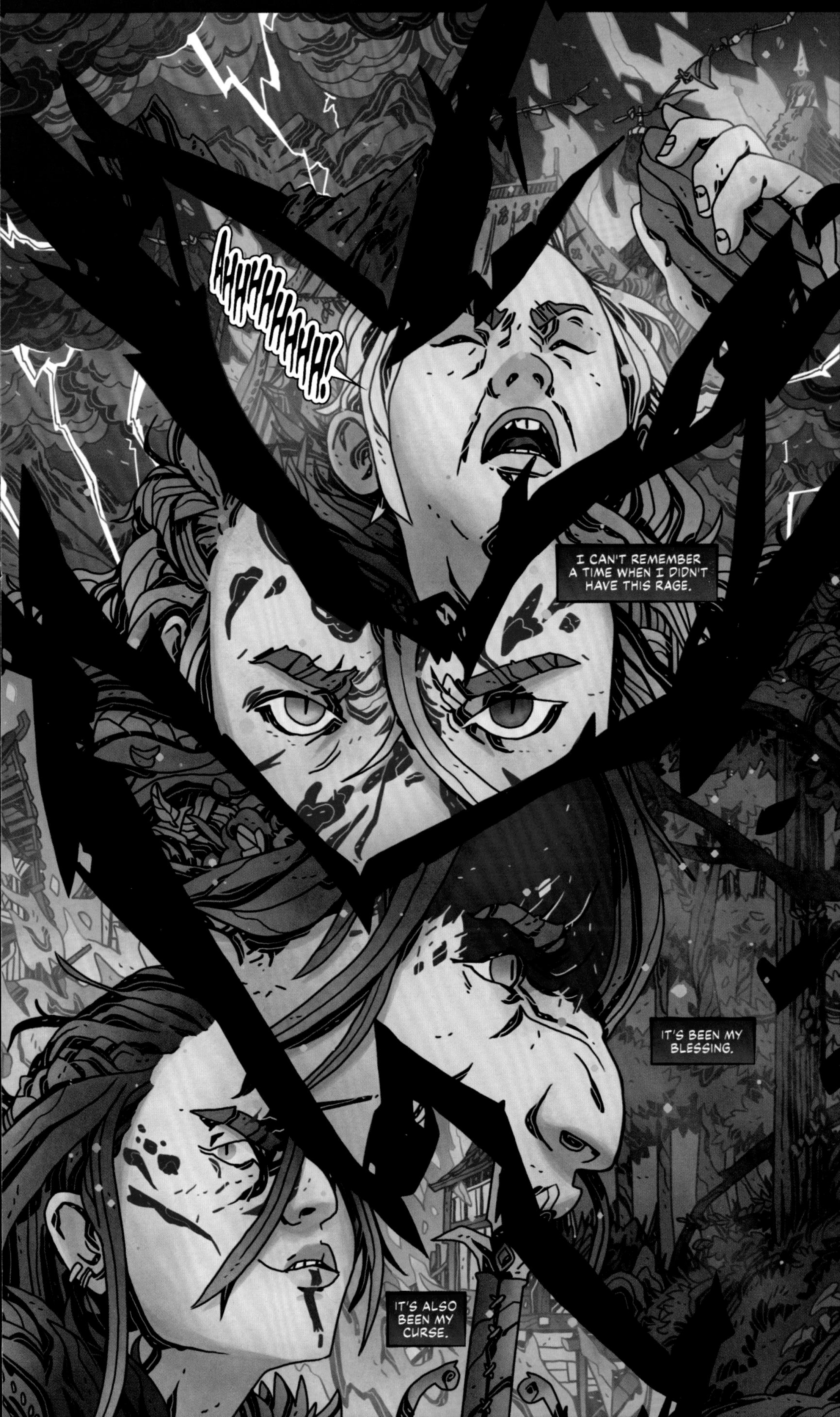
AHHHHHHHHH!
I CAN'T REMEMBER A TIME WHEN I DIDN'T HAVE THIS RAGE.
IT'S BEEN MY BLESSING.
IT'S ALSO BEEN MY CURSE.

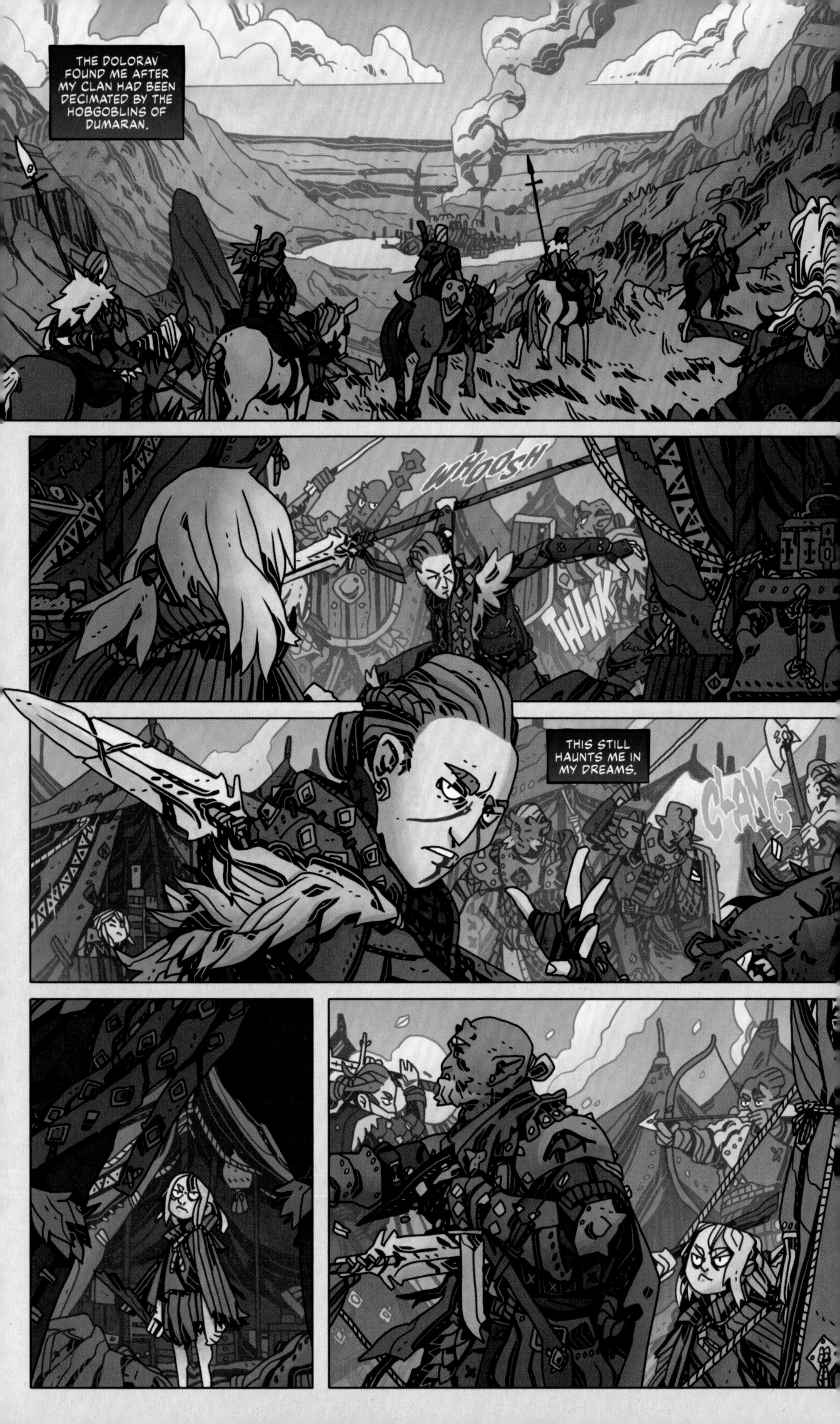
THE DOLORAV FOUND ME AFTER MY CLAN HAD BEEN DECIMATED BY THE HOBGOBLINS OF DUMARAN.
WHOOSH
THUNK
THIS STILL HAUNTS ME IN MY DREAMS.
CLANG

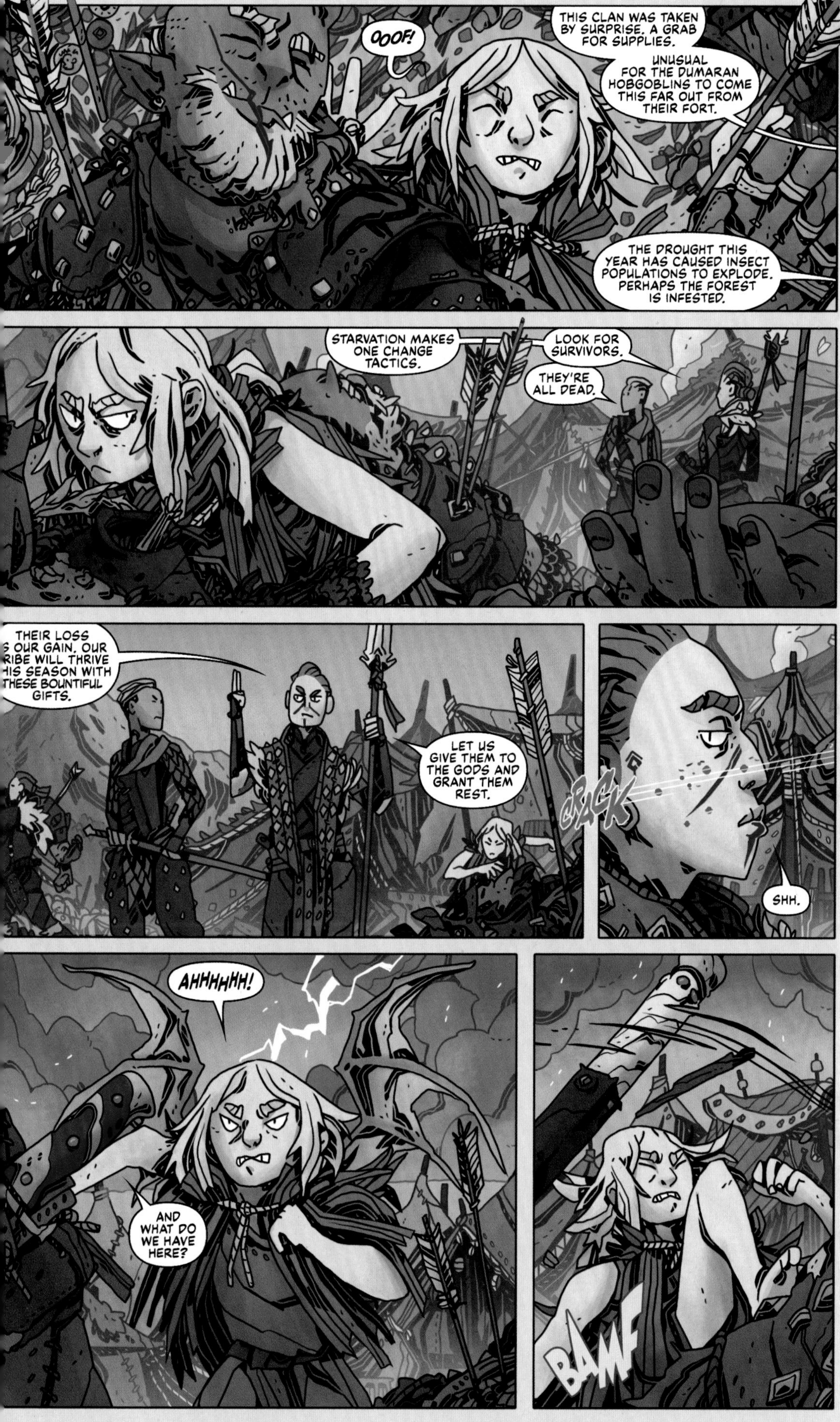
OOOF!
THIS CLAN WAS TAKEN BY SURPRISE. A GRAB FOR SUPPLIES.
UNUSUAL FOR THE DUMARAN HOBGOBLINS TO COME THIS FAR OUT FROM THEIR FORT.
THE DROUGHT THIS YEAR HAS CAUSED INSECT POPULATIONS TO EXPLODE. PERHAPS THE FOREST IS INFESTED.
STARVATION MAKES ONE CHANGE TACTICS.
LOOK FOR SURVIVORS.
THEY'RE ALL DEAD.
THEIR LOSS S OUR GAIN. OUR RIBE WILL THRIVE HIS SEASON WITH THESE BOUNTIFUL GIFTS.
LET US GIVE THEM TO THE GODS AND GRANT THEM REST.
CRACK
SHH.
AHHHHHH!
AND WHAT DO WE HAVE HERE?
BAMF

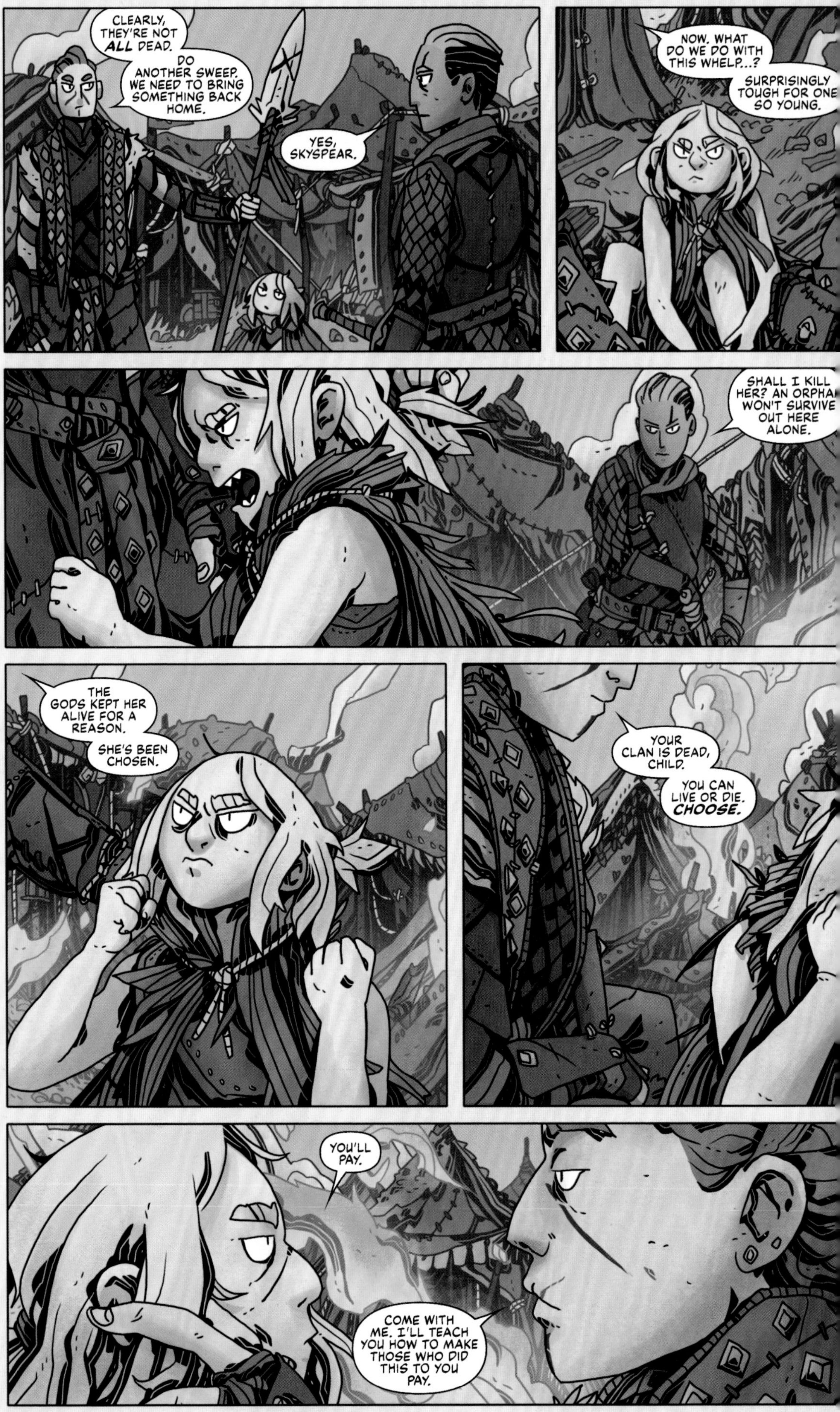
CLEARLY, THEY'RE NOT ALL DEAD.
DO ANOTHER SWEEP. WE NEED TO BRING SOMETHING BACK HOME.
YES, SKYSPEAR.
NOW, WHAT DO WE DO WITH THIS WHELP...?
SURPRISINGLY TOUGH FOR ONE SO YOUNG.
SHALL I KILL HER? AN ORPHA WON'T SURVIVE OUT HERE ALONE.
THE GODS KEPT HER ALIVE FOR A REASON.
SHE'S BEEN CHOSEN.
YOUR CLAN IS DEAD, CHILD.
YOU CAN LIVE OR DIE. CHOOSE.
YOU'LL PAY.
COME WITH ME. I'LL TEACH YOU HOW TO MAKE THOSE WHO DID THIS TO YOU PAY.

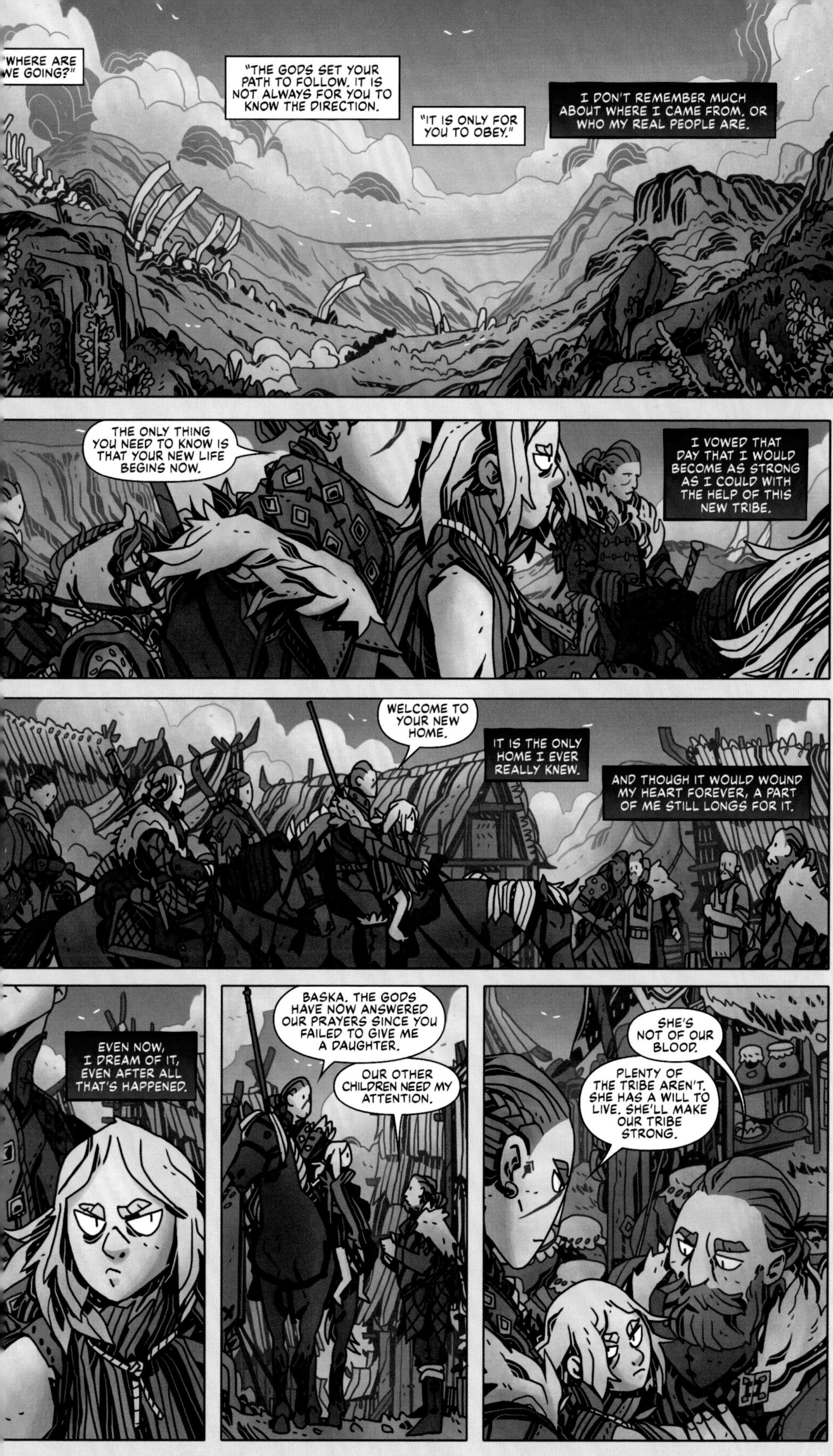

"WHERE ARE WE GOING?"
"THE GODS SET YOUR PATH TO FOLLOW. IT IS NOT ALWAYS FOR YOU TO KNOW THE DIRECTION.
"IT IS ONLY FOR YOU TO OBEY."
I DON'T REMEMBER MUCH ABOUT WHERE I CAME FROM, OR WHO MY REAL PEOPLE ARE.
THE ONLY THING YOU NEED TO KNOW IS THAT YOUR NEW LIFE BEGINS NOW.
I VOWED THAT DAY THAT I WOULD BECOME AS STRONG AS I COULD WITH THE HELP OF THIS NEW TRIBE.
WELCOME TO YOUR NEW HOME.
IT IS THE ONLY HOME I EVER REALLY KNEW.
AND THOUGH IT WOULD WOUND MY HEART FOREVER, A PART OF ME STILL LONGS FOR IT.
EVEN NOW, I DREAM OF IT, EVEN AFTER ALL THAT'S HAPPENED.
BASKA. THE GODS HAVE NOW ANSWERED OUR PRAYERS SINCE YOU FAILED TO GIVE ME A DAUGHTER.
OUR OTHER CHILDREN NEED MY ATTENTION.
SHE'S NOT OF OUR BLOOD.
PLENTY OF THE TRIBE AREN'T. SHE HAS A WILL TO LIVE. SHE'LL MAKE OUR TRIBE STRONG.

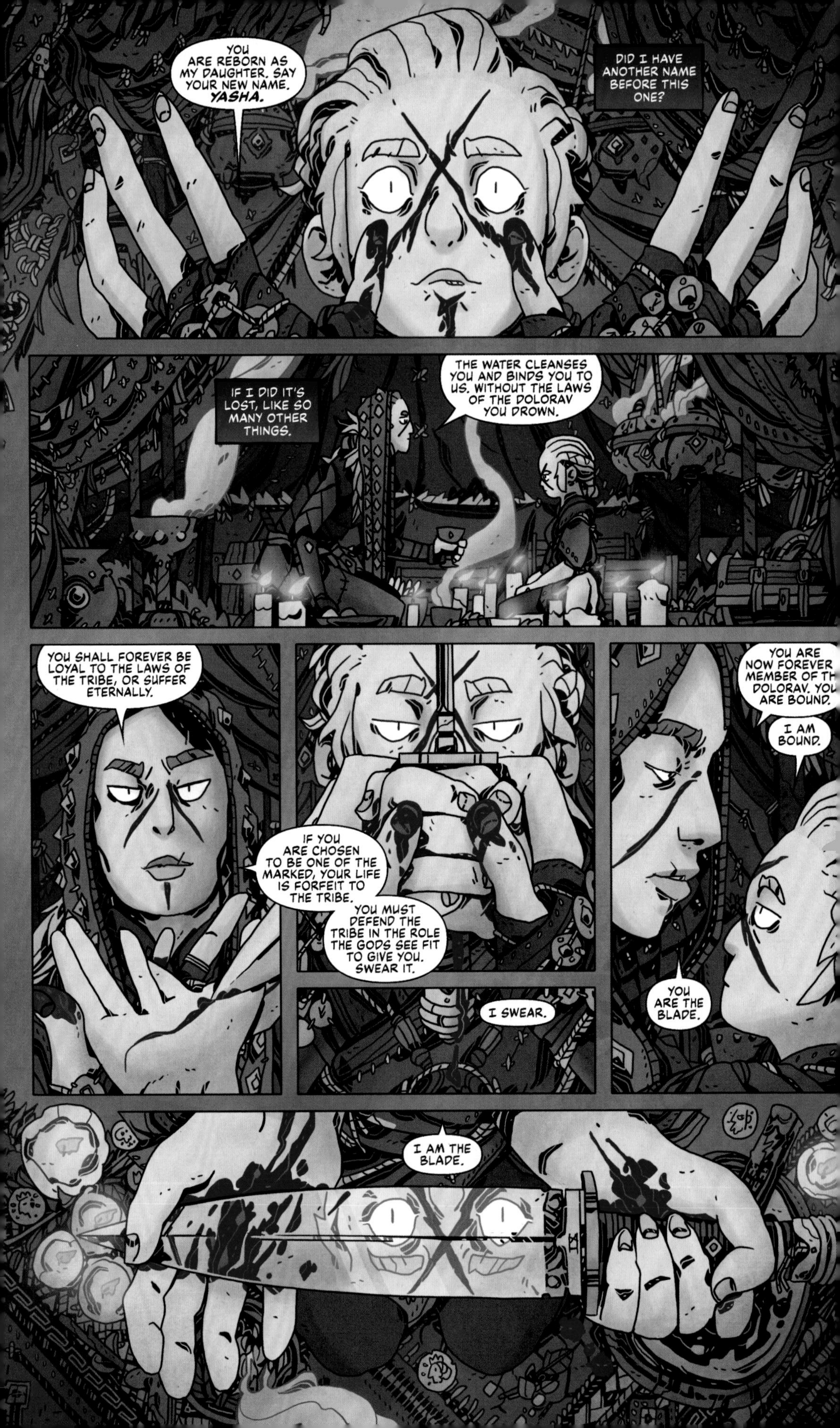

YOU ARE REBORN AS MY DAUGHTER. SAY YOUR NEW NAME. YASHA.
DID I HAVE ANOTHER NAME BEFORE THIS ONE?
IF I DID IT'S LOST, LIKE SO MANY OTHER THINGS.
THE WATER CLEANSES YOU AND BINDS YOU TO US. WITHOUT THE LAWS OF THE DOLORAV YOU DROWN.
YOU SHALL FOREVER BE LOYAL TO THE LAWS OF THE TRIBE, OR SUFFER ETERNALLY.
IF YOU ARE CHOSEN TO BE ONE OF THE MARKED, YOUR LIFE IS FORFEIT TO THE TRIBE.
YOU MUST DEFEND THE TRIBE IN THE ROLE THE GODS SEE FIT TO GIVE YOU. SWEAR IT.
I SWEAR.
YOU ARE NOW FOREVER MEMBER OF TH DOLORAV. YOU ARE BOUND.
I AM BOUND.
YOU ARE THE BLADE.
I AM THE BLADE.

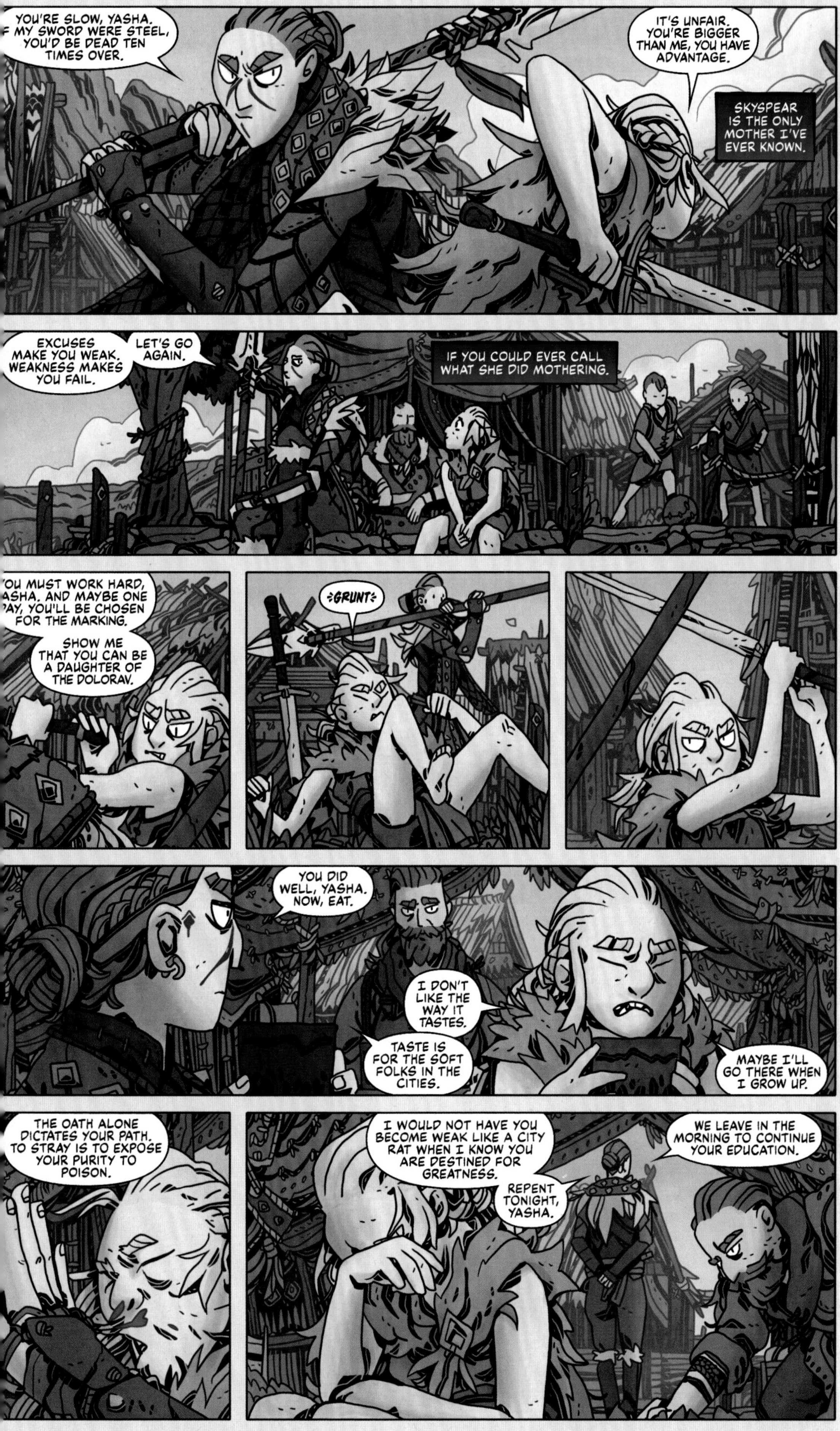
YOU'RE SLOW, YASHA. IF MY SWORD WERE STEEL, YOU'D BE DEAD TEN TIMES OVER.
IT'S UNFAIR. YOU'RE BIGGER THAN ME, YOU HAVE ADVANTAGE.
SKYSPEAR IS THE ONLY MOTHER I'VE EVER KNOWN.
EXCUSES MAKE YOU WEAK. WEAKNESS MAKES YOU FAIL.
LET'S GO AGAIN.
IF YOU COULD EVER CALL WHAT SHE DID MOTHERING.
YOU MUST WORK HARD, YASHA. AND MAYBE ONE DAY, YOU'LL BE CHOSEN FOR THE MARKING.
SHOW ME THAT YOU CAN BE A DAUGHTER OF THE DOLORAV.
GRUNT
YOU DID WELL, YASHA. NOW, EAT.
I DON'T LIKE THE WAY IT TASTES.
TASTE IS FOR THE SOFT FOLKS IN THE CITIES.
MAYBE I'LL GO THERE WHEN I GROW UP.
THE OATH ALONE DICTATES YOUR PATH. TO STRAY IS TO EXPOSE YOUR PURITY TO POISON.
I WOULD NOT HAVE YOU BECOME WEAK LIKE A CITY RAT WHEN I KNOW YOU ARE DESTINED FOR GREATNESS.
REPENT TONIGHT, YASHA.
WE LEAVE IN THE MORNING TO CONTINUE YOUR EDUCATION.

APOLOGIES FOR BEING SLOW.

HUNGER BITES AT MY BONES AFTER HOURS OF WALKING. THE GODS TEST ME ALREADY.

YOU DON'T YET KNOW WHAT HUNGER IS.

BUT YOU'L LEARI

DO NOT MOVE FROM THIS CIRCLE UNTIL I RETURN. IF YOU DO, I WILL KNOW.

IF YOU DO, YOU ARE EXILED.

YES, SKYSPEAR.

SKYSPEAR AND THE TRIBE WERE MY WHOLE WORLD. I WOULD DO ANYTHING THAT SHE ASKED.

THE AGONY OF LIVING ALONE WITHOUT THE TRIBE KEPT ME IN PLACE.

BUT I WA TERRIFIE

I SAT UNMOVING. THE SUN ROSE AND FELL SEVEN TIMES.

WHAT IS THAT?

MEAT. WHEN WE ARE HUNGRY, WE DO NOT JUDGE. WE EAT WHATEVER WE CAN.

IF YOU'RE TO LEAD, REMEMBER THE PEOPLE EAT FIRST. YOU EAT LAST. YOU EAT SCRAPS.

TO DO THAT, HUNGER MUST BECOME YOUR OLD FRIEND.

I WON' FORGE SKYSPEA

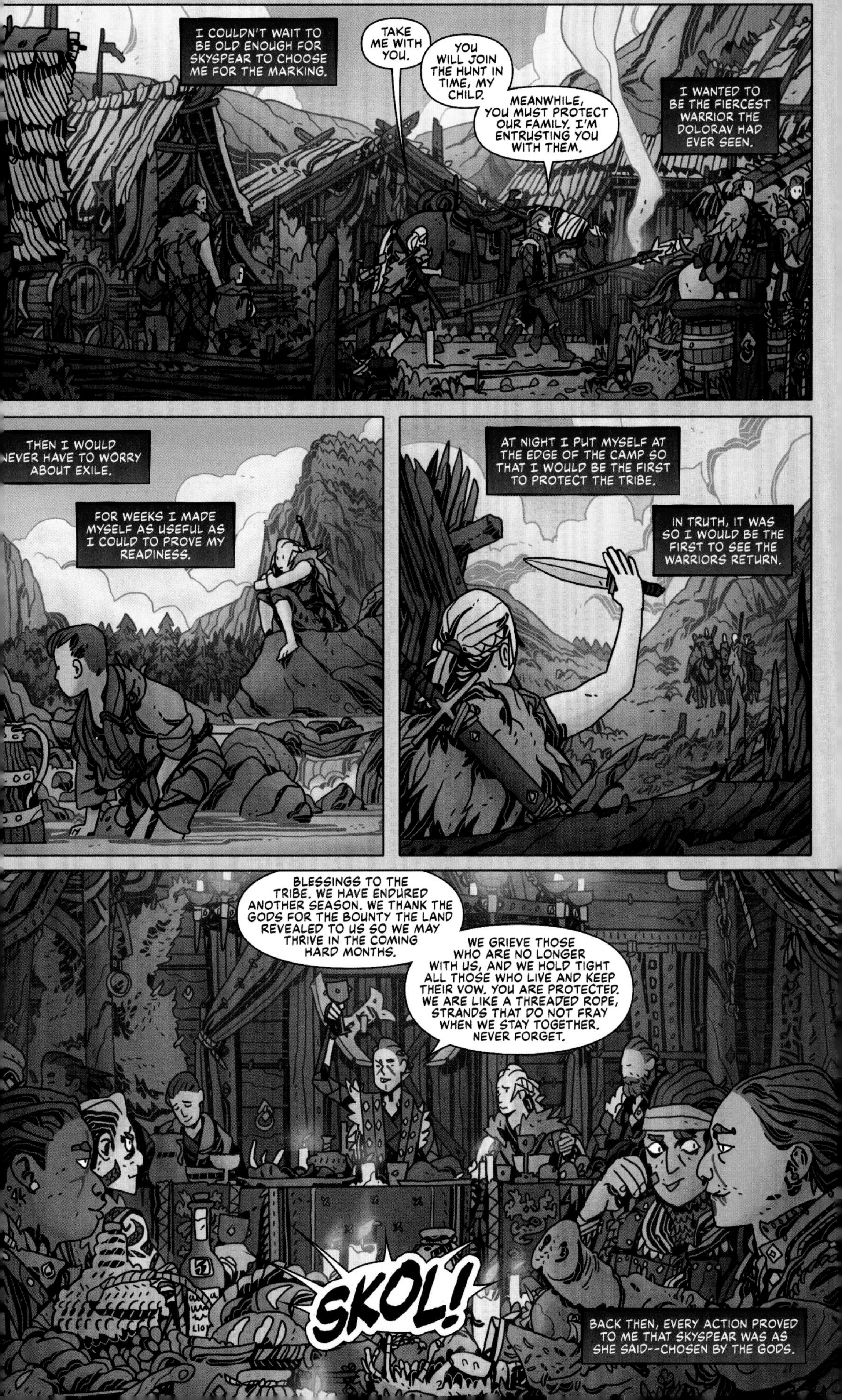
I COULDN'T WAIT TO BE OLD ENOUGH FOR SKYSPEAR TO CHOOSE ME FOR THE MARKING.
TAKE ME WITH YOU.
YOU WILL JOIN THE HUNT IN TIME, MY CHILD.
MEANWHILE, YOU MUST PROTECT OUR FAMILY. I'M ENTRUSTING YOU WITH THEM.
I WANTED TO BE THE FIERCEST WARRIOR THE DOLORAV HAD EVER SEEN.
THEN I WOULD NEVER HAVE TO WORRY ABOUT EXILE.
FOR WEEKS I MADE MYSELF AS USEFUL AS I COULD TO PROVE MY READINESS.
AT NIGHT I PUT MYSELF AT THE EDGE OF THE CAMP SO THAT I WOULD BE THE FIRST TO PROTECT THE TRIBE.
IN TRUTH, IT WAS SO I WOULD BE THE FIRST TO SEE THE WARRIORS RETURN.
BLESSINGS TO THE TRIBE. WE HAVE ENDURED ANOTHER SEASON. WE THANK THE GODS FOR THE BOUNTY THE LAND REVEALED TO US SO WE MAY THRIVE IN THE COMING HARD MONTHS.
WE GRIEVE THOSE WHO ARE NO LONGER WITH US, AND WE HOLD TIGHT ALL THOSE WHO LIVE AND KEEP THEIR VOW. YOU ARE PROTECTED. WE ARE LIKE A THREADED ROPE, STRANDS THAT DO NOT FRAY WHEN WE STAY TOGETHER. NEVER FORGET.
SKOL!
BACK THEN, EVERY ACTION PROVED TO ME THAT SKYSPEAR WAS AS SHE SAID--CHOSEN BY THE GODS.

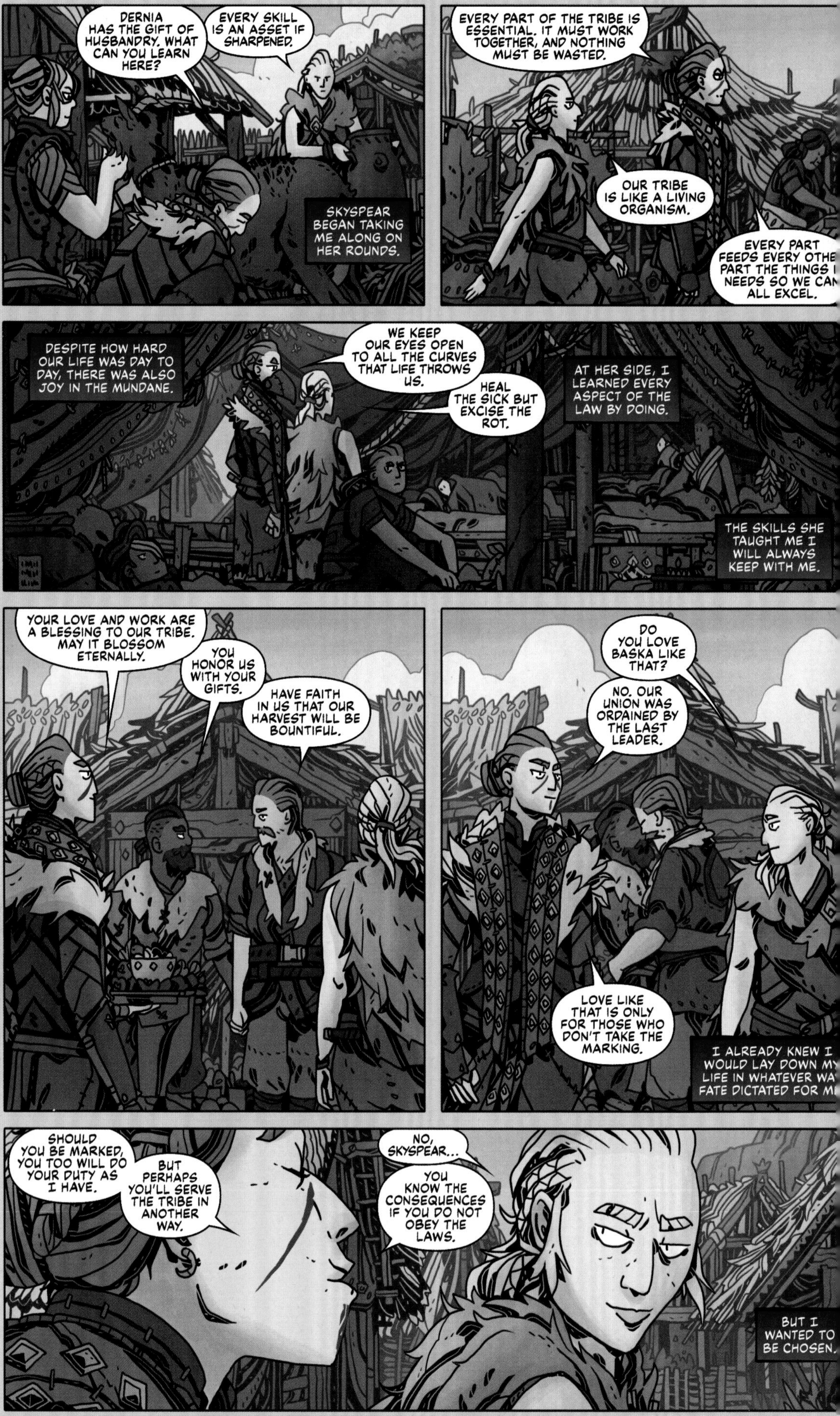
DERNIA HAS THE GIFT OF HUSBANDRY. WHAT CAN YOU LEARN HERE?
EVERY SKILL IS AN ASSET IF SHARPENED.
SKYSPEAR BEGAN TAKING ME ALONG ON HER ROUNDS.
EVERY PART OF THE TRIBE IS ESSENTIAL. IT MUST WORK TOGETHER, AND NOTHING MUST BE WASTED.
OUR TRIBE IS LIKE A LIVING ORGANISM.
EVERY PART FEEDS EVERY OTHE PART THE THINGS I NEEDS SO WE CAN ALL EXCEL.
DESPITE HOW HARD OUR LIFE WAS DAY TO DAY, THERE WAS ALSO JOY IN THE MUNDANE.
WE KEEP OUR EYES OPEN TO ALL THE CURVES THAT LIFE THROWS US.
HEAL THE SICK BUT EXCISE THE ROT.
AT HER SIDE, I LEARNED EVERY ASPECT OF THE LAW BY DOING.
THE SKILLS SHE TAUGHT ME I WILL ALWAYS KEEP WITH ME.
YOUR LOVE AND WORK ARE A BLESSING TO OUR TRIBE. MAY IT BLOSSOM ETERNALLY.
YOU HONOR US WITH YOUR GIFTS.
HAVE FAITH IN US THAT OUR HARVEST WILL BE BOUNTIFUL.
DO YOU LOVE BASKA LIKE THAT?
NO. OUR UNION WAS ORDAINED BY THE LAST LEADER.
LOVE LIKE THAT IS ONLY FOR THOSE WHO DON'T TAKE THE MARKING.
I ALREADY KNEW I WOULD LAY DOWN MY LIFE IN WHATEVER WA FATE DICTATED FOR M
SHOULD YOU BE MARKED, YOU TOO WILL DO YOUR DUTY AS I HAVE.
BUT PERHAPS YOU'LL SERVE THE TRIBE IN ANOTHER WAY.
NO, SKYSPEAR...
YOU KNOW THE CONSEQUENCES IF YOU DO NOT OBEY THE LAWS.
BUT I WANTED TO BE CHOSEN.

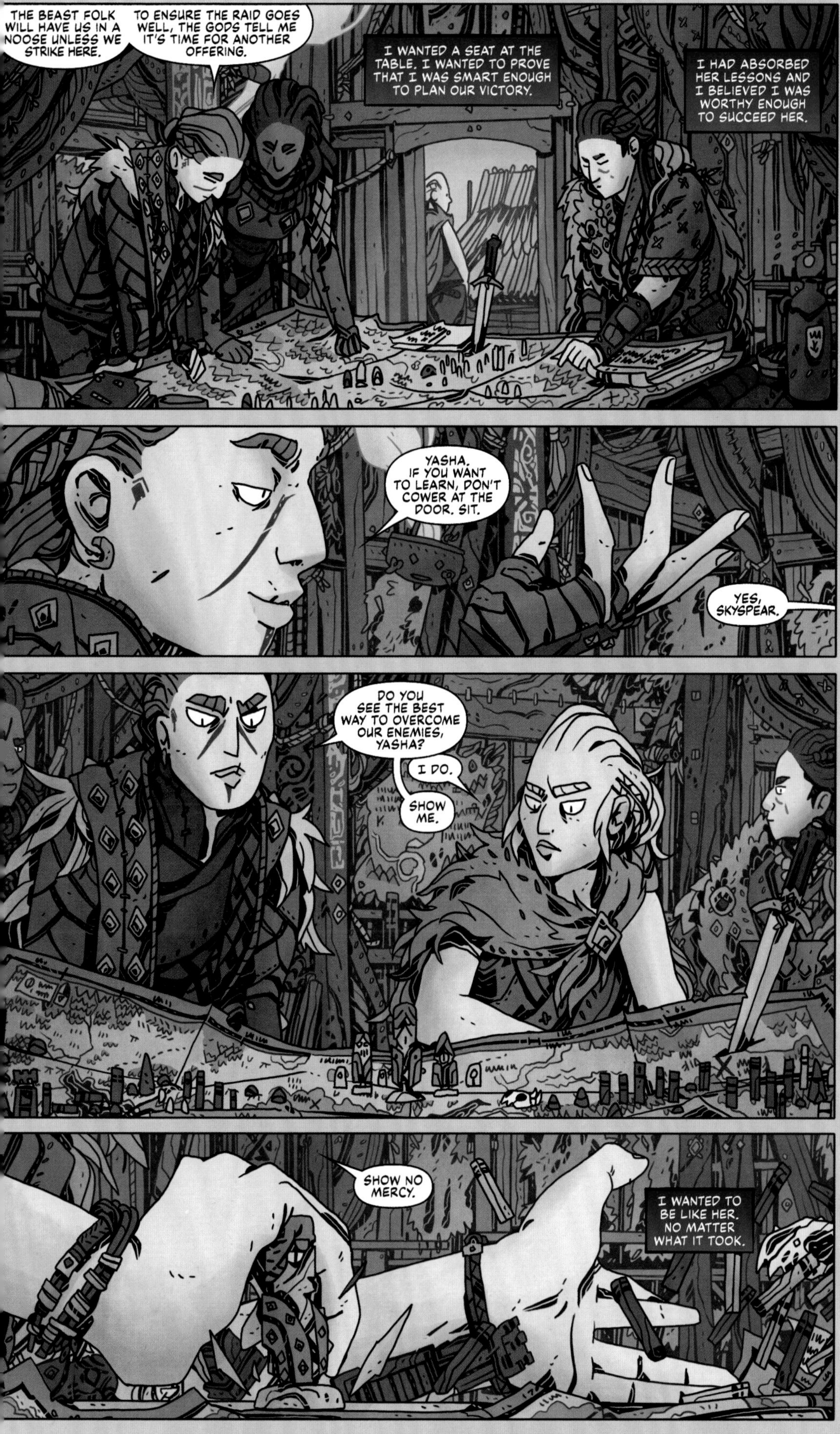
THE BEAST FOLK WILL HAVE US IN A NOOSE UNLESS WE STRIKE HERE.
TO ENSURE THE RAID GOES WELL, THE GODS TELL ME IT'S TIME FOR ANOTHER OFFERING.
I WANTED A SEAT AT THE TABLE. I WANTED TO PROVE THAT I WAS SMART ENOUGH TO PLAN OUR VICTORY.
I HAD ABSORBED HER LESSONS AND I BELIEVED I WAS WORTHY ENOUGH TO SUCCEED HER.
YASHA. IF YOU WANT TO LEARN, DON'T COWER AT THE DOOR. SIT.
YES, SKYSPEAR.
DO YOU SEE THE BEST WAY TO OVERCOME OUR ENEMIES, YASHA?
I DO.
SHOW ME.
SHOW NO MERCY.
I WANTED TO BE LIKE HER. NO MATTER WHAT IT TOOK.

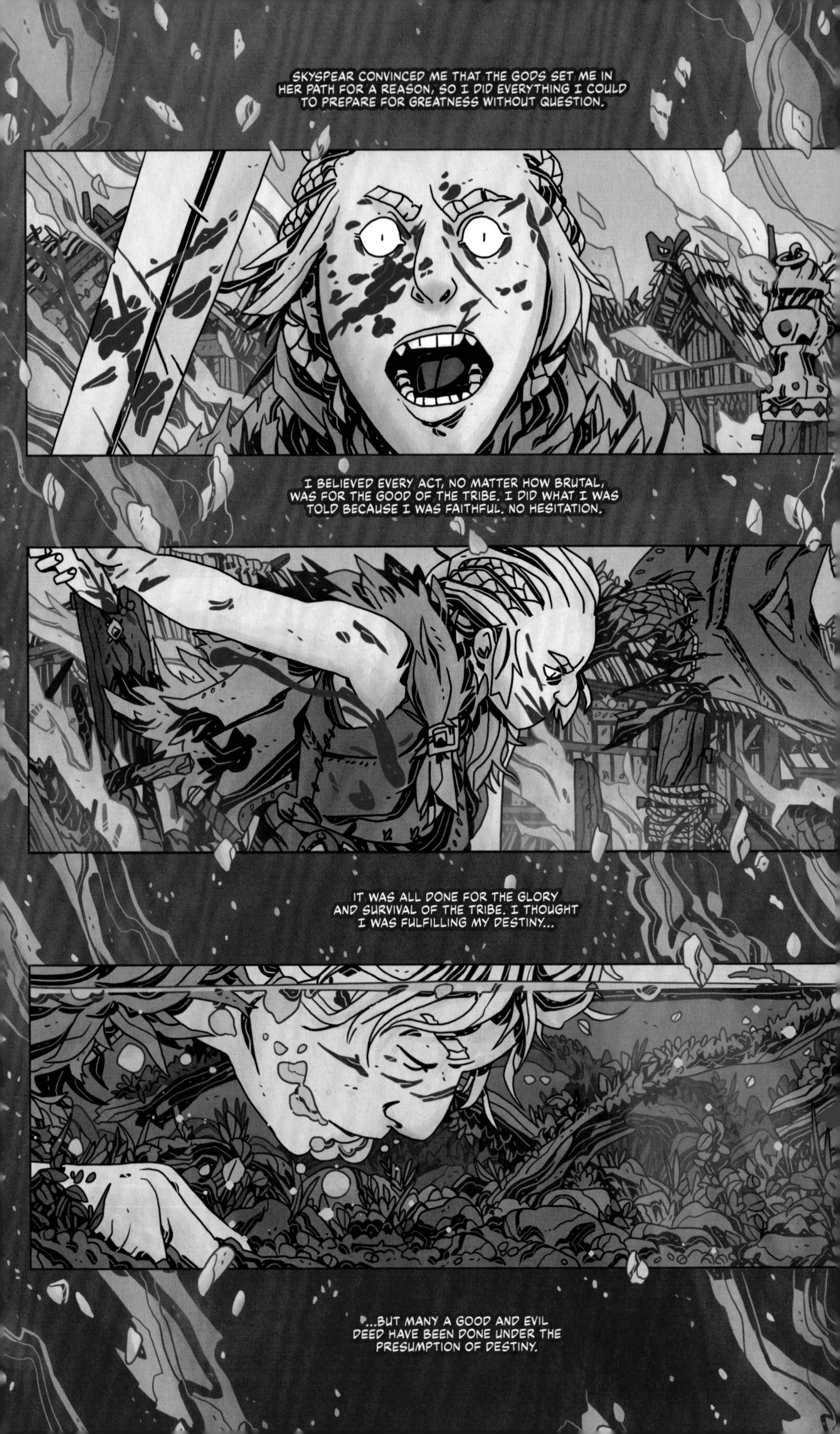
SKYSPEAR CONVINCED ME THAT THE GODS SET ME IN HER PATH FOR A REASON, SO I DID EVERYTHING I COULD TO PREPARE FOR GREATNESS WITHOUT QUESTION.
I BELIEVED EVERY ACT, NO MATTER HOW BRUTAL, WAS FOR THE GOOD OF THE TRIBE. I DID WHAT I WAS TOLD BECAUSE I WAS FAITHFUL. NO HESITATION.
IT WAS ALL DONE FOR THE GLORY AND SURVIVAL OF THE TRIBE. I THOUGHT I WAS FULFILLING MY DESTINY...
...BUT MANY A GOOD AND EVIL DEED HAVE BEEN DONE UNDER THE PRESUMPTION OF DESTINY.

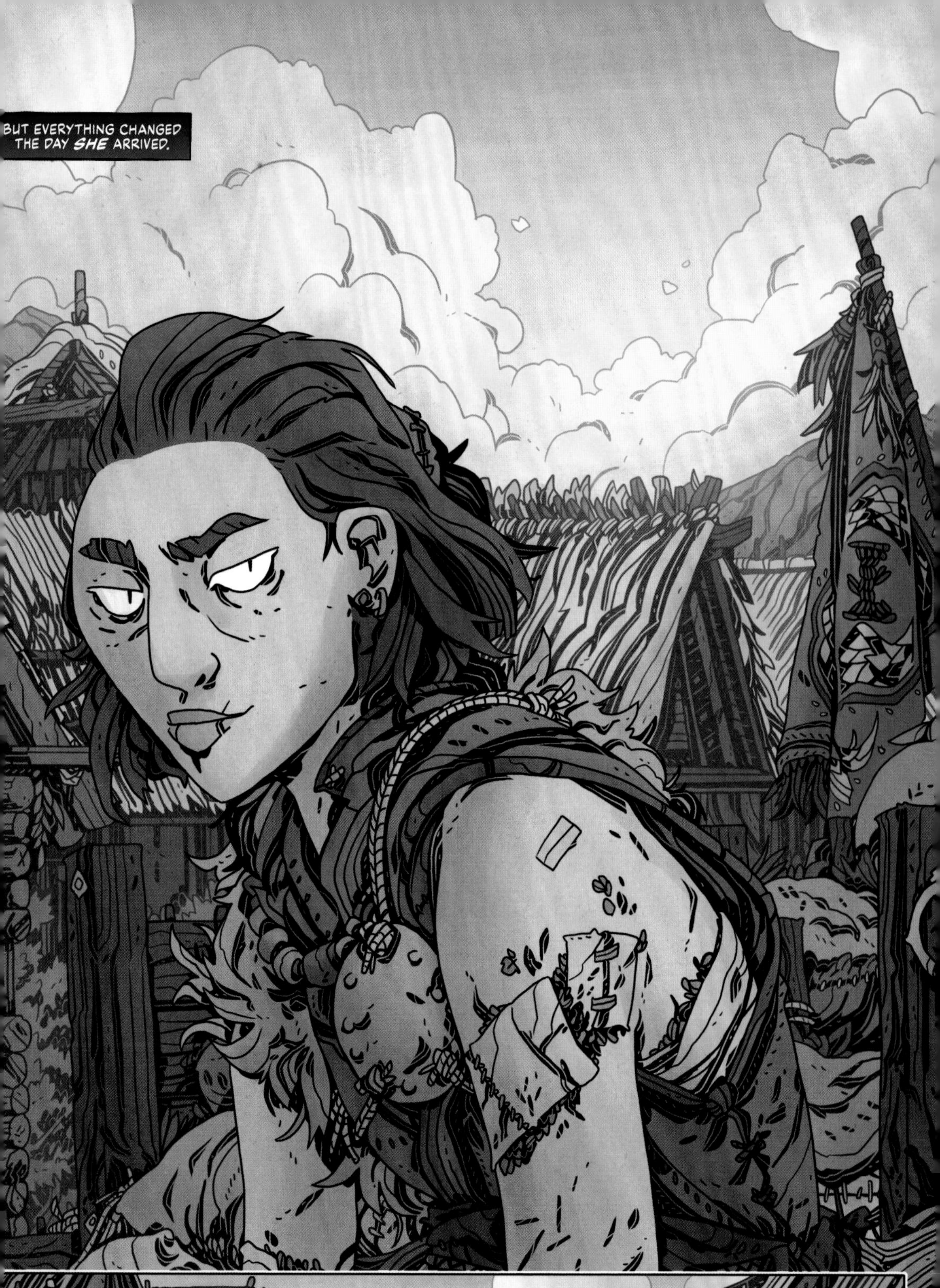
BUT EVERYTHING CHANGED THE DAY SHE ARRIVED.

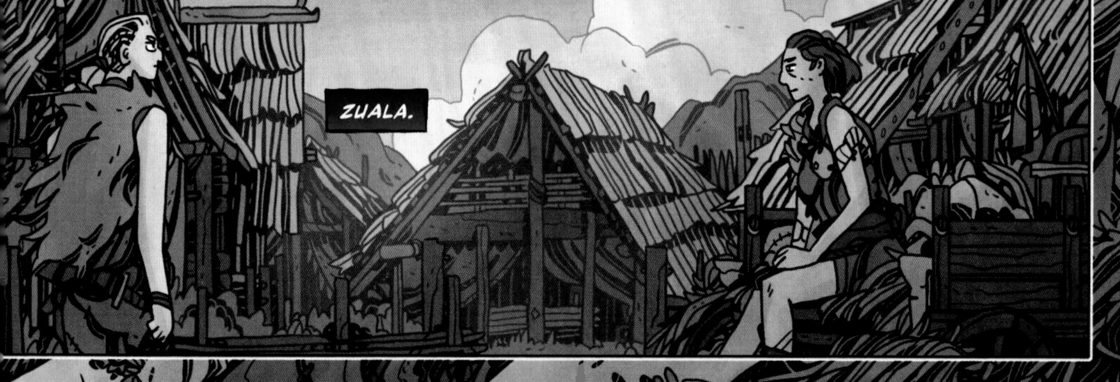
ZUALA.

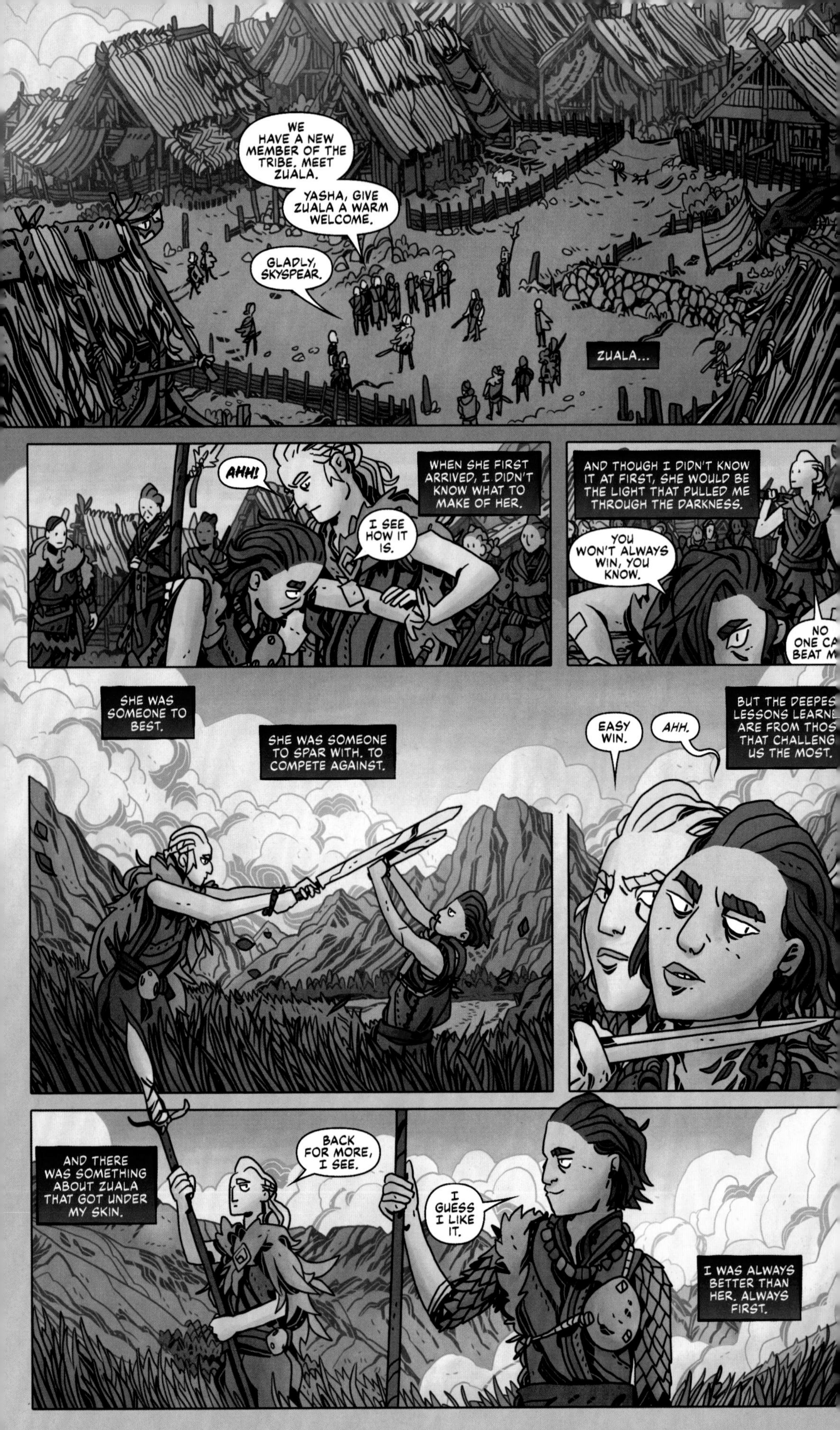
WE HAVE A NEW MEMBER OF THE TRIBE. MEET ZUALA.
YASHA, GIVE ZUALA A WARM WELCOME.
GLADLY, SKYSPEAR.
ZUALA...
AHH!
WHEN SHE FIRST ARRIVED, I DIDN'T KNOW WHAT TO MAKE OF HER.
I SEE HOW IT IS.
AND THOUGH I DIDN'T KNOW IT AT FIRST, SHE WOULD BE THE LIGHT THAT PULLED ME THROUGH THE DARKNESS.
YOU WON'T ALWAYS WIN, YOU KNOW.
SHE WAS SOMEONE TO BEST.
SHE WAS SOMEONE TO SPAR WITH. TO COMPETE AGAINST.
EASY WIN.
AHH.
AND THERE WAS SOMETHING ABOUT ZUALA THAT GOT UNDER MY SKIN.
BACK FOR MORE, I SEE.
I GUESS I LIKE IT.
I WAS ALWAYS BETTER THAN HER. ALWAYS FIRST.

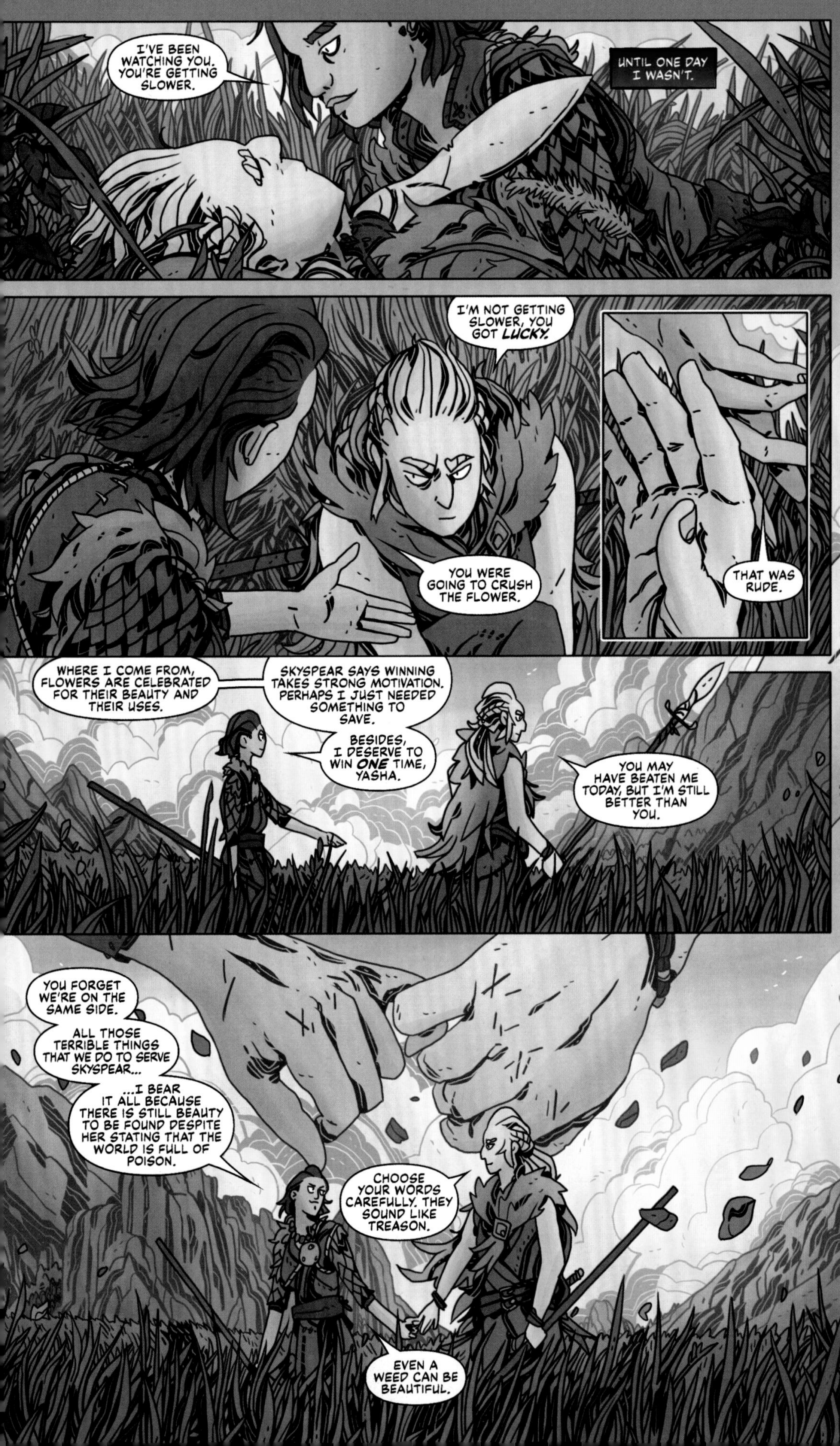
UNTIL ONE DAY I WASN'T.
I'VE BEEN WATCHING YOU. YOU'RE GETTING SLOWER.
I'M NOT GETTING SLOWER, YOU GOT LUCKY.
YOU WERE GOING TO CRUSH THE FLOWER.
THAT WAS RUDE.
WHERE I COME FROM, FLOWERS ARE CELEBRATED FOR THEIR BEAUTY AND THEIR USES.
SKYSPEAR SAYS WINNING TAKES STRONG MOTIVATION. PERHAPS I JUST NEEDED SOMETHING TO SAVE.
BESIDES, I DESERVE TO WIN ONE TIME, YASHA.
YOU MAY HAVE BEATEN ME TODAY, BUT I'M STILL BETTER THAN YOU.
YOU FORGET WE'RE ON THE SAME SIDE.
ALL THOSE TERRIBLE THINGS THAT WE DO TO SERVE SKYSPEAR...
...I BEAR IT ALL BECAUSE THERE IS STILL BEAUTY TO BE FOUND DESPITE HER STATING THAT THE WORLD IS FULL OF POISON.
CHOOSE YOUR WORDS CAREFULLY. THEY SOUND LIKE TREASON.
EVEN A WEED CAN BE BEAUTIFUL.

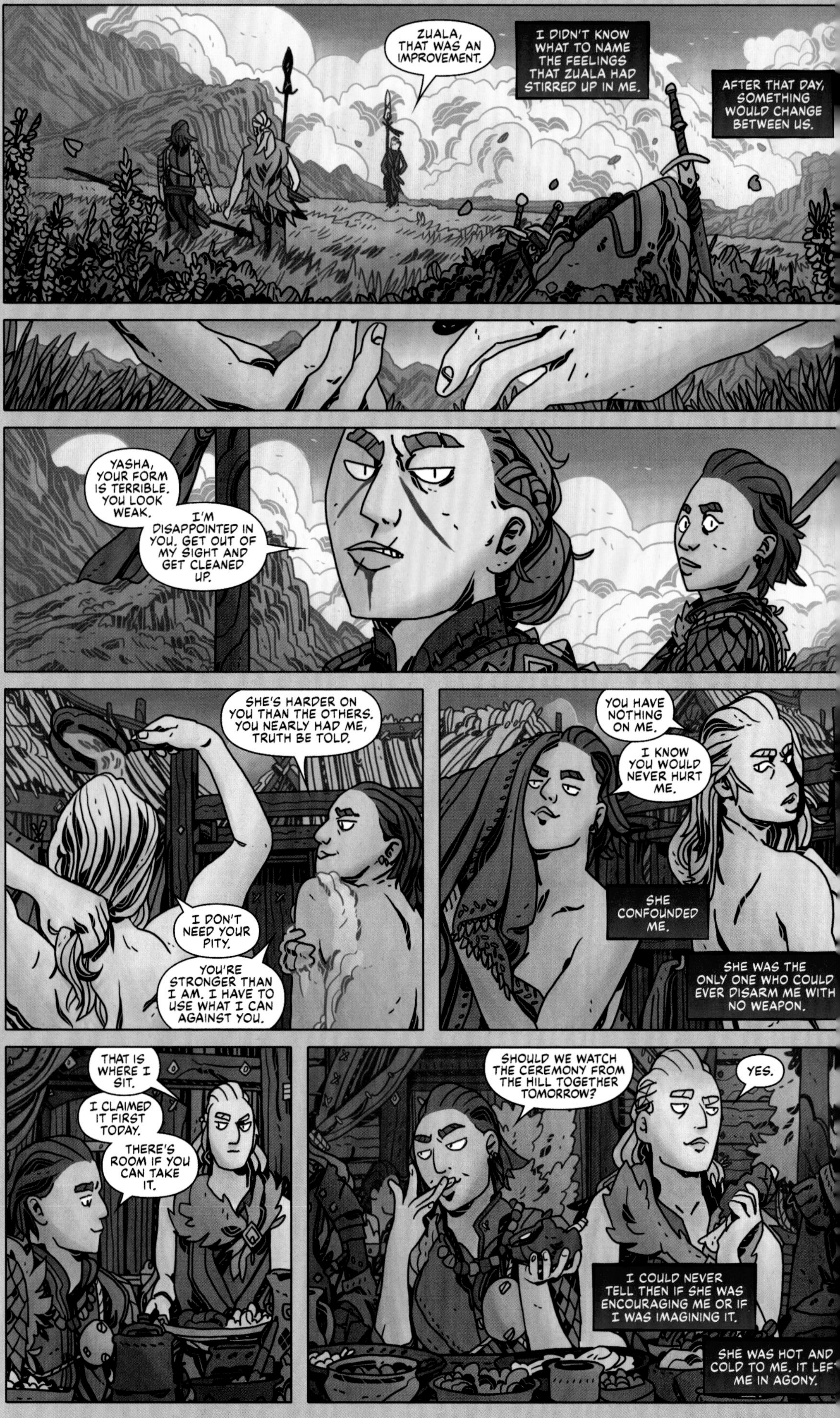
ZUALA, THAT WAS AN IMPROVEMENT.
I DIDN'T KNOW WHAT TO NAME THE FEELINGS THAT ZUALA HAD STIRRED UP IN ME.
AFTER THAT DAY, SOMETHING WOULD CHANGE BETWEEN US.
YASHA, YOUR FORM IS TERRIBLE. YOU LOOK WEAK.
I'M DISAPPOINTED IN YOU. GET OUT OF MY SIGHT AND GET CLEANED UP.
SHE'S HARDER ON YOU THAN THE OTHERS. YOU NEARLY HAD ME, TRUTH BE TOLD.
I DON'T NEED YOUR PITY.
YOU'RE STRONGER THAN I AM. I HAVE TO USE WHAT I CAN AGAINST YOU.
YOU HAVE NOTHING ON ME.
I KNOW YOU WOULD NEVER HURT ME.
SHE CONFOUNDED ME.
SHE WAS THE ONLY ONE WHO COULD EVER DISARM ME WITH NO WEAPON.
THAT IS WHERE I SIT.
I CLAIMED IT FIRST TODAY.
THERE'S ROOM IF YOU CAN TAKE IT.
SHOULD WE WATCH THE CEREMONY FROM THE HILL TOGETHER TOMORROW?
YES.
I COULD NEVER TELL THEN IF SHE WAS ENCOURAGING ME OR IF I WAS IMAGINING IT.
SHE WAS HOT AND COLD TO ME. IT LEF ME IN AGONY.

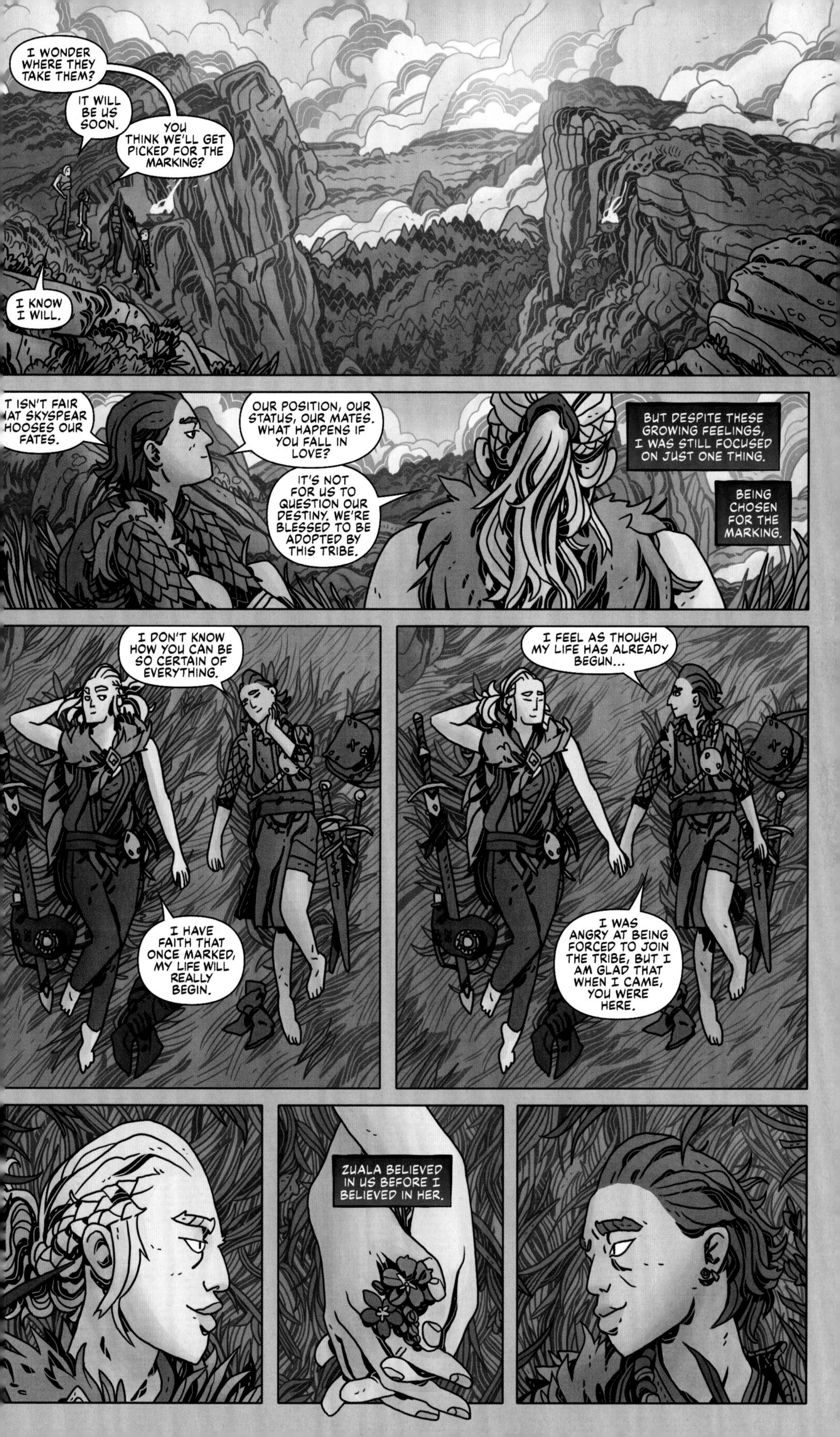
I WONDER WHERE THEY TAKE THEM?
IT WILL BE US SOON.
YOU THINK WE'LL GET PICKED FOR THE MARKING?
I KNOW I WILL.
T ISN'T FAIR IAT SKYSPEAR HOOSES OUR FATES.
OUR POSITION, OUR STATUS, OUR MATES. WHAT HAPPENS IF YOU FALL IN LOVE?
IT'S NOT FOR US TO QUESTION OUR DESTINY. WE'RE BLESSED TO BE ADOPTED BY THIS TRIBE.
BUT DESPITE THESE GROWING FEELINGS, I WAS STILL FOCUSED ON JUST ONE THING.
BEING CHOSEN FOR THE MARKING.
I DON'T KNOW HOW YOU CAN BE SO CERTAIN OF EVERYTHING.
I HAVE FAITH THAT ONCE MARKED, MY LIFE WILL REALLY BEGIN.
I FEEL AS THOUGH MY LIFE HAS ALREADY BEGUN...
I WAS ANGRY AT BEING FORCED TO JOIN THE TRIBE, BUT I AM GLAD THAT WHEN I CAME, YOU WERE HERE.
ZUALA BELIEVED IN US BEFORE I BELIEVED IN HER.

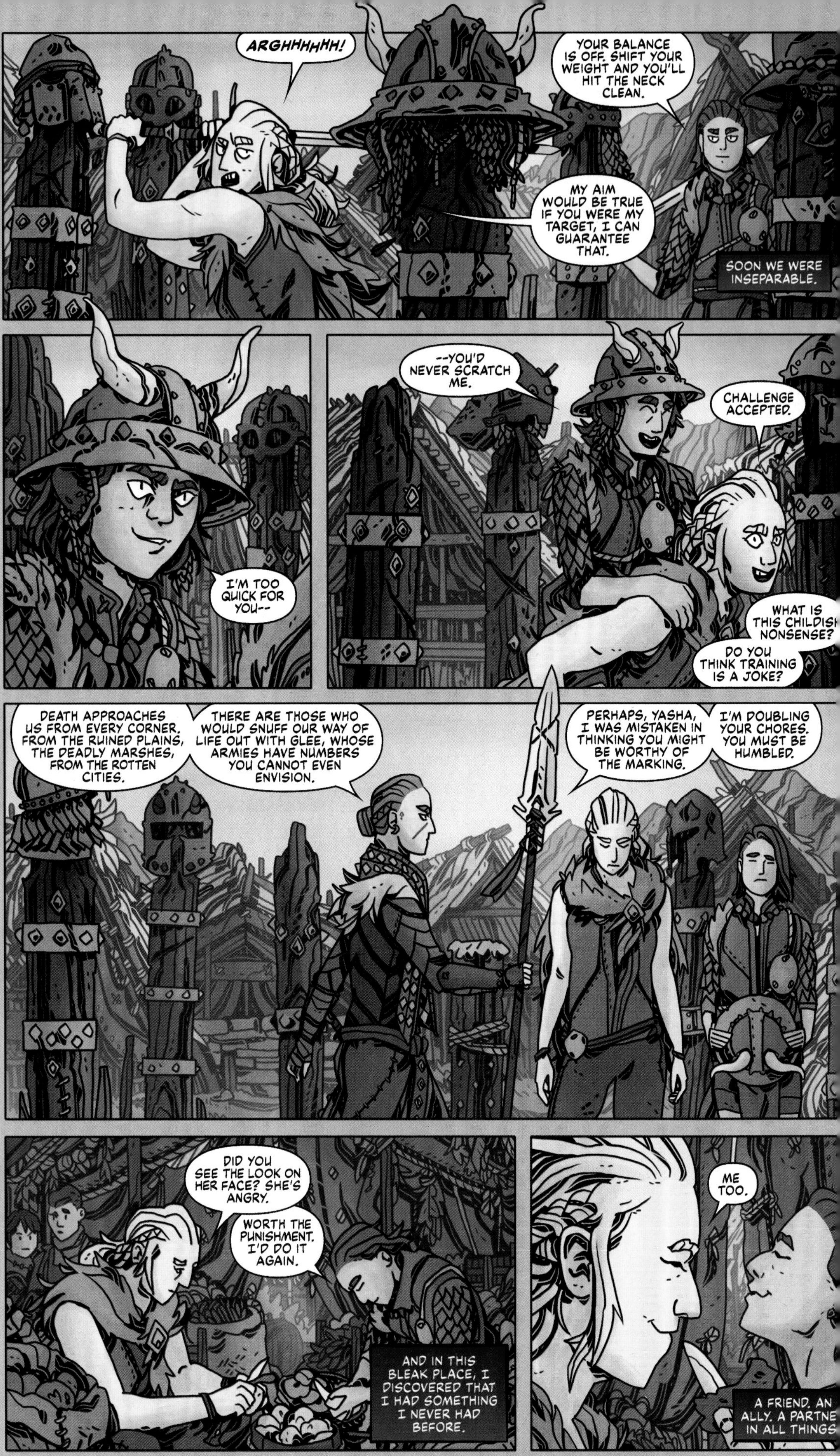
ARGHHHHHH!
YOUR BALANCE IS OFF. SHIFT YOUR WEIGHT AND YOU'LL HIT THE NECK CLEAN.
MY AIM WOULD BE TRUE IF YOU WERE MY TARGET, I CAN GUARANTEE THAT.
SOON WE WERE INSEPARABLE.
I'M TOO QUICK FOR YOU--
--YOU'D NEVER SCRATCH ME.
CHALLENGE ACCEPTED.
WHAT IS THIS CHILDISH NONSENSE?
DO YOU THINK TRAINING IS A JOKE?
DEATH APPROACHES US FROM EVERY CORNER. FROM THE RUINED PLAINS, THE DEADLY MARSHES, FROM THE ROTTEN CITIES.
THERE ARE THOSE WHO WOULD SNUFF OUR WAY OF LIFE OUT WITH GLEE, WHOSE ARMIES HAVE NUMBERS YOU CANNOT EVEN ENVISION.
PERHAPS, YASHA, I WAS MISTAKEN IN THINKING YOU MIGHT BE WORTHY OF THE MARKING.
I'M DOUBLING YOUR CHORES. YOU MUST BE HUMBLED.
DID YOU SEE THE LOOK ON HER FACE? SHE'S ANGRY.
WORTH THE PUNISHMENT. I'D DO IT AGAIN.
AND IN THIS BLEAK PLACE, I DISCOVERED THAT I HAD SOMETHING I NEVER HAD BEFORE.
ME TOO.
A FRIEND. AN ALLY. A PARTNER IN ALL THINGS.

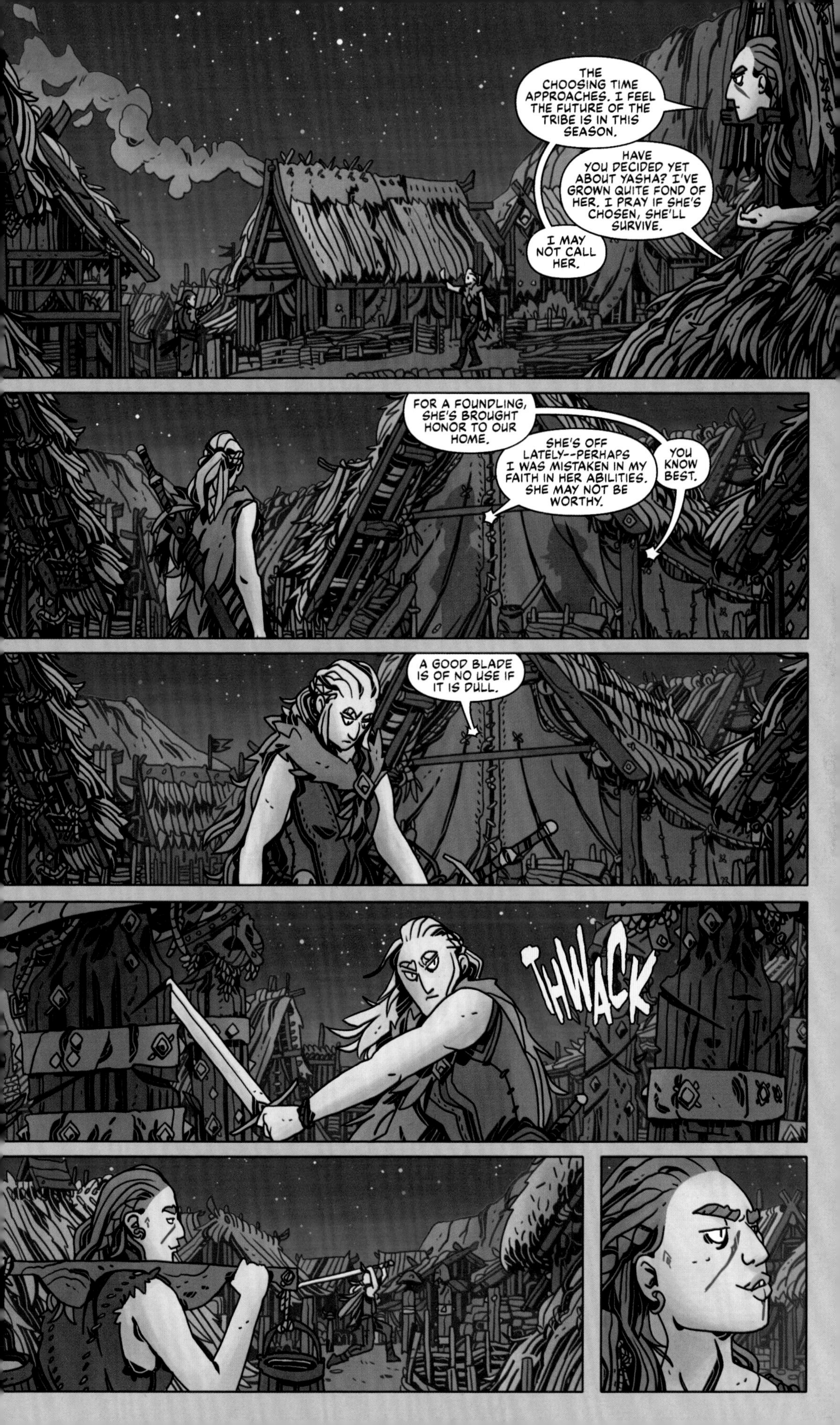
THE CHOOSING TIME APPROACHES. I FEEL THE FUTURE OF THE TRIBE IS IN THIS SEASON.
I MAY NOT CALL HER.
HAVE YOU DECIDED YET ABOUT YASHA? I'VE GROWN QUITE FOND OF HER. I PRAY IF SHE'S CHOSEN, SHE'LL SURVIVE.
FOR A FOUNDLING, SHE'S BROUGHT HONOR TO OUR HOME.
SHE'S OFF LATELY--PERHAPS I WAS MISTAKEN IN MY FAITH IN HER ABILITIES. SHE MAY NOT BE WORTHY.
YOU KNOW BEST.
A GOOD BLADE IS OF NO USE IF IT IS DULL.
THWACK

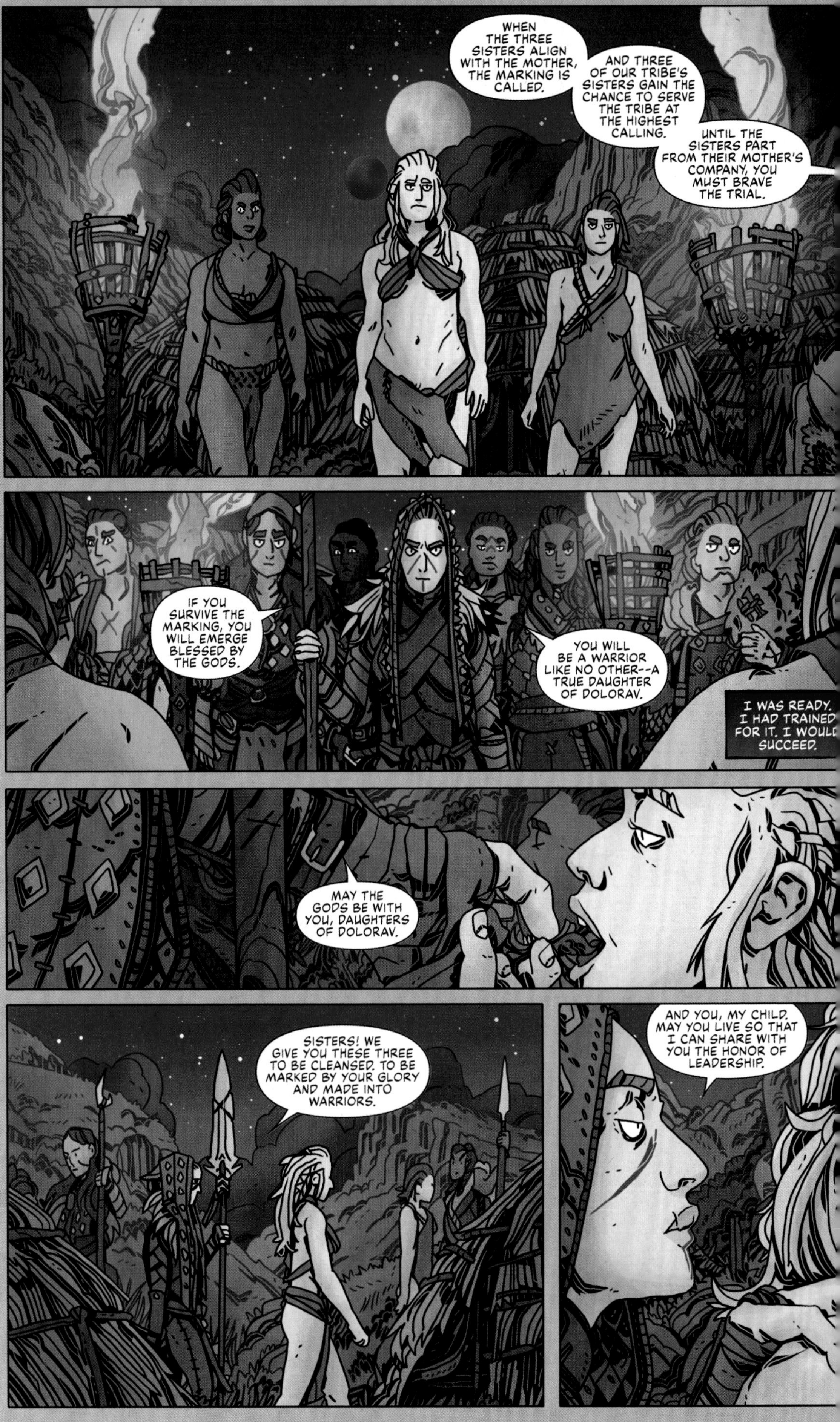
WHEN THE THREE SISTERS ALIGN WITH THE MOTHER, THE MARKING IS CALLED.
AND THREE OF OUR TRIBE'S SISTERS GAIN THE CHANCE TO SERVE THE TRIBE AT THE HIGHEST CALLING.
UNTIL THE SISTERS PART FROM THEIR MOTHER'S COMPANY, YOU MUST BRAVE THE TRIAL.
IF YOU SURVIVE THE MARKING, YOU WILL EMERGE BLESSED BY THE GODS.
YOU WILL BE A WARRIOR LIKE NO OTHER--A TRUE DAUGHTER OF DOLORAV.
I WAS READY. I HAD TRAINED FOR IT. I WOULD SUCCEED.
MAY THE GODS BE WITH YOU, DAUGHTERS OF DOLORAV.
SISTERS! WE GIVE YOU THESE THREE TO BE CLEANSED. TO BE MARKED BY YOUR GLORY AND MADE INTO WARRIORS.
AND YOU, MY CHILD. MAY YOU LIVE SO THAT I CAN SHARE WITH YOU THE HONOR OF LEADERSHIP.

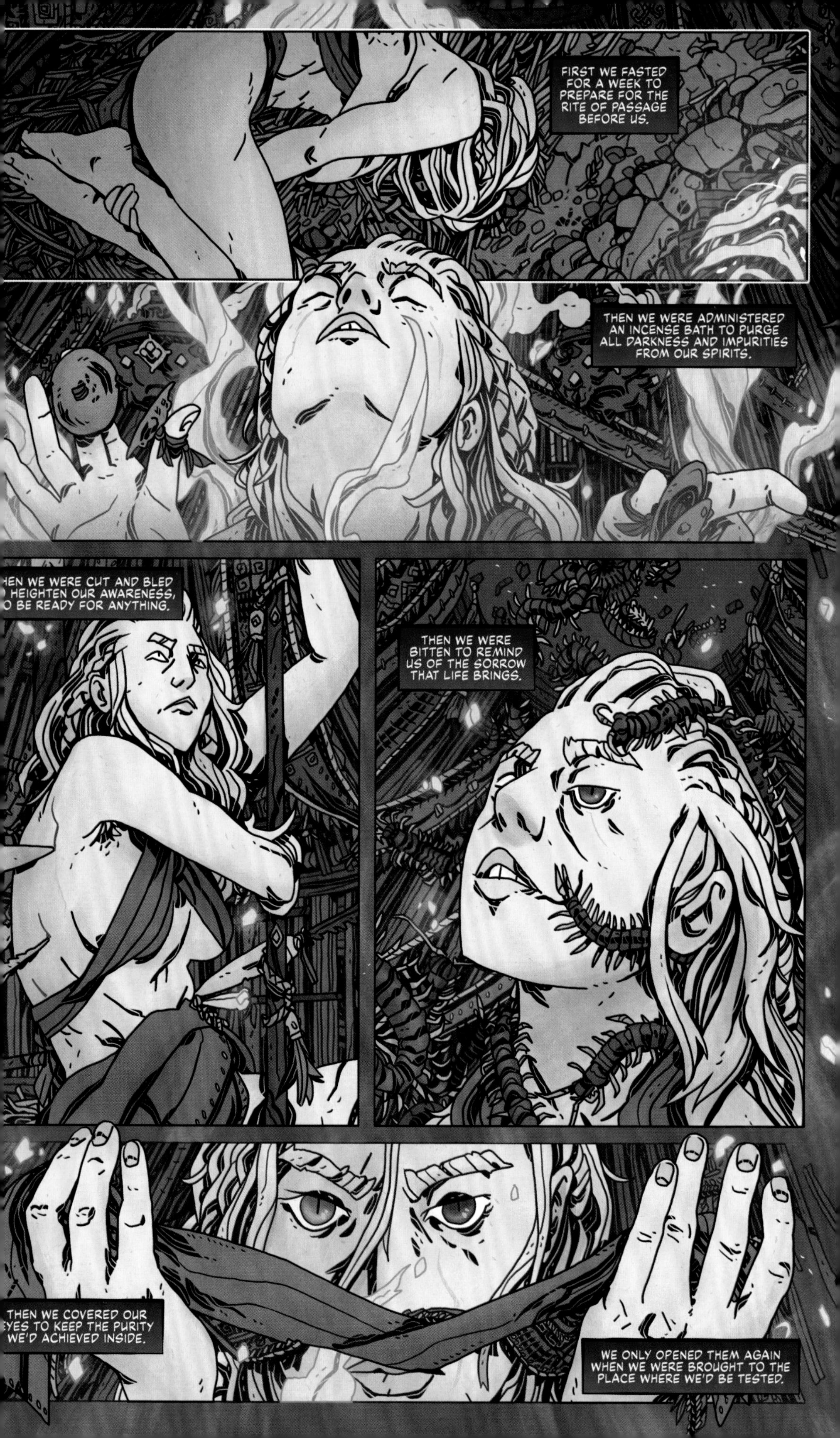
FIRST WE FASTED FOR A WEEK TO PREPARE FOR THE RITE OF PASSAGE BEFORE US.
THEN WE WERE ADMINISTERED AN INCENSE BATH TO PURGE ALL DARKNESS AND IMPURITIES FROM OUR SPIRITS.
HEN WE WERE CUT AND BLED
HEIGHTEN OUR AWARENESS,
O BE READY FOR ANYTHING.
THEN WE WERE BITTEN TO REMIND US OF THE SORROW THAT LIFE BRINGS.
THEN WE COVERED OUR
YES TO KEEP THE PURITY
WE'D ACHIEVED INSIDE.
WE ONLY OPENED THEM AGAIN WHEN WE WERE BROUGHT TO THE PLACE WHERE WE'D BE TESTED.

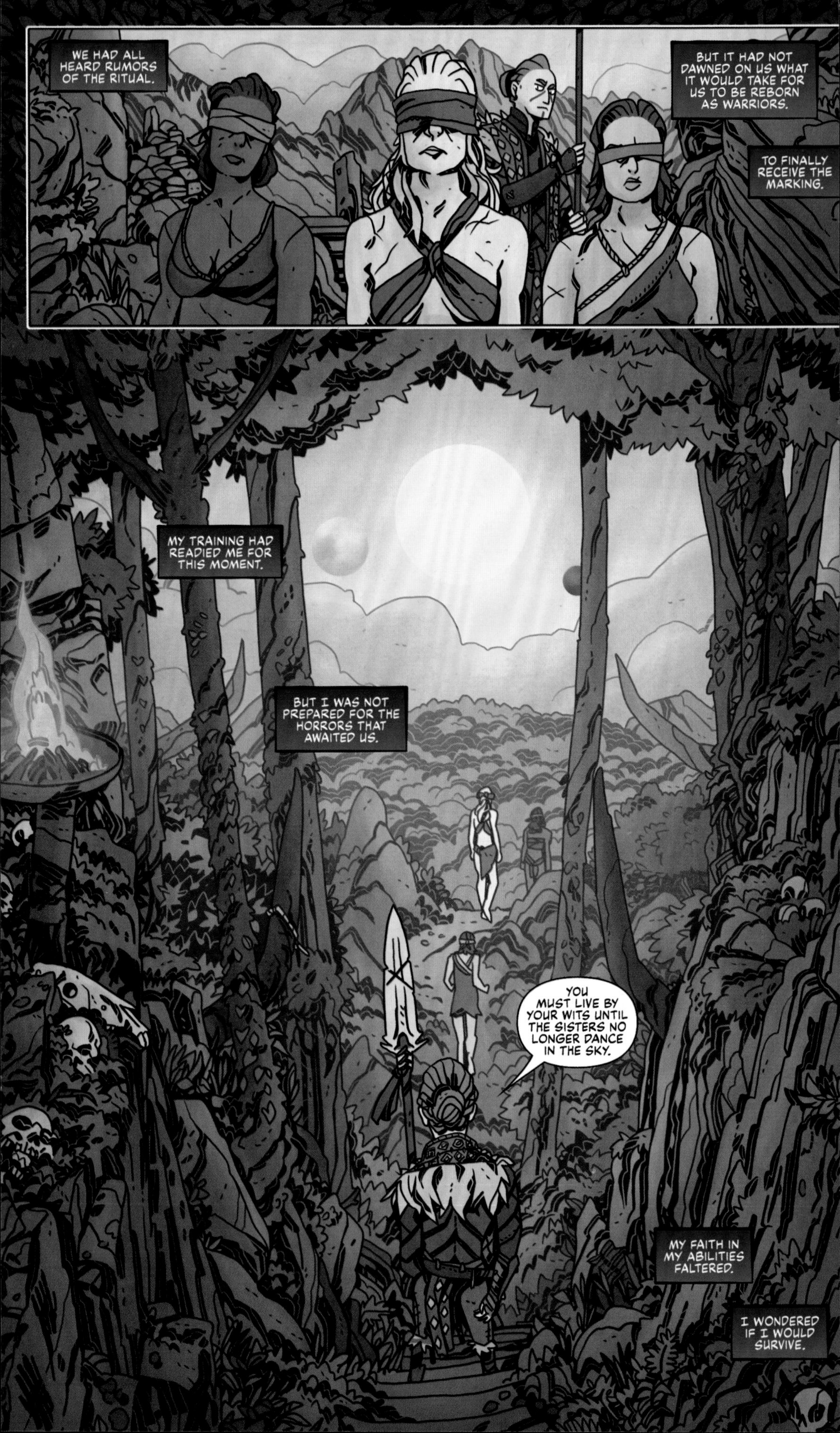
WE HAD ALL HEARD RUMORS OF THE RITUAL.
BUT IT HAD NOT DAWNED ON US WHAT IT WOULD TAKE FOR US TO BE REBORN AS WARRIORS.
TO FINALLY RECEIVE THE MARKING.
MY TRAINING HAD READIED ME FOR THIS MOMENT.
BUT I WAS NOT PREPARED FOR THE HORRORS THAT AWAITED US.
YOU MUST LIVE BY YOUR WITS UNTIL THE SISTERS NO LONGER DANCE IN THE SKY.
MY FAITH IN MY ABILITIES FALTERED.
I WONDERED IF I WOULD SURVIVE.

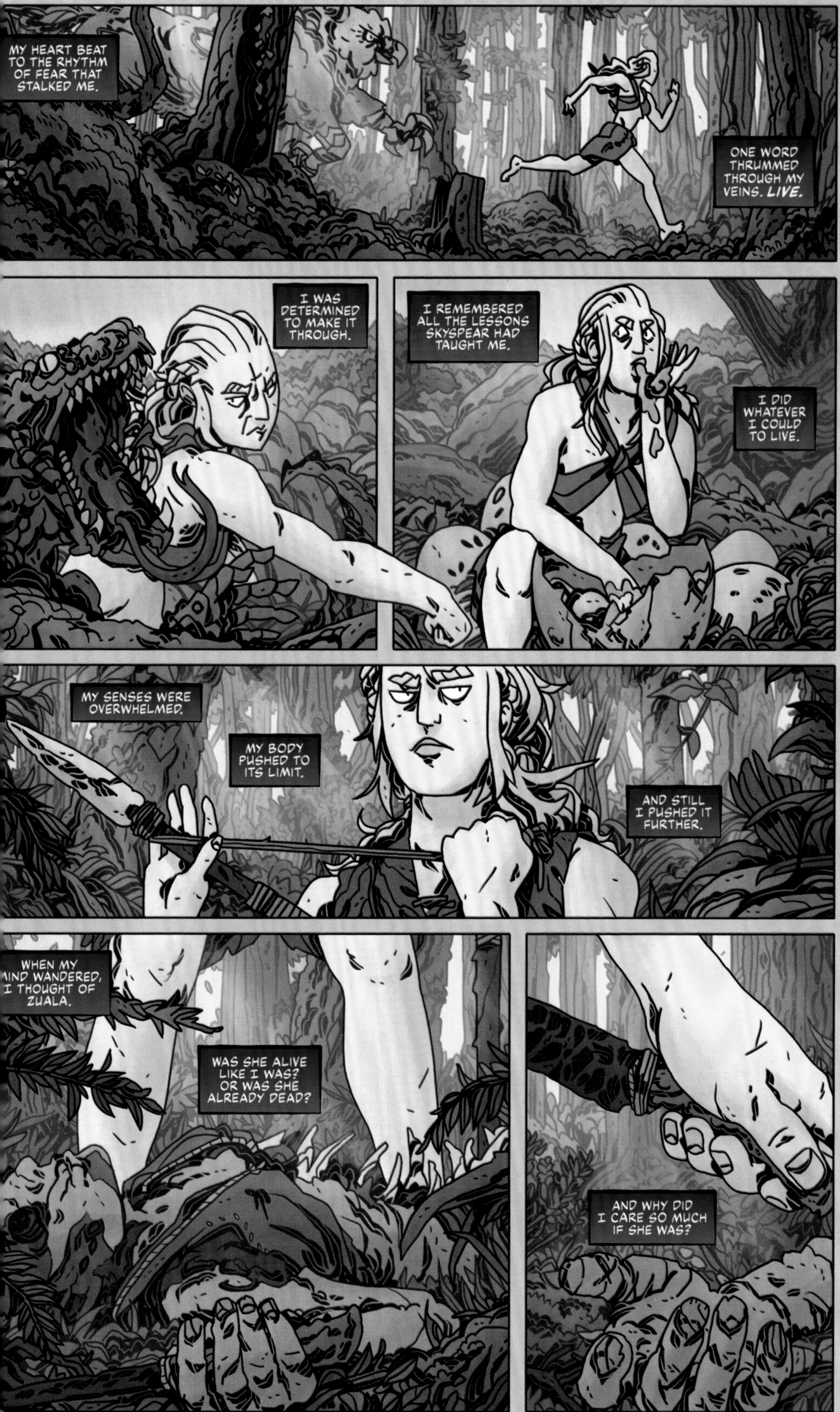
MY HEART BEAT TO THE RHYTHM OF FEAR THAT STALKED ME.
ONE WORD THRUMMED THROUGH MY VEINS. LIVE.
I WAS DETERMINED TO MAKE IT THROUGH.
I REMEMBERED ALL THE LESSONS SKYSPEAR HAD TAUGHT ME.
I DID WHATEVER I COULD TO LIVE.
MY SENSES WERE OVERWHELMED.
MY BODY PUSHED TO ITS LIMIT.
AND STILL I PUSHED IT FURTHER.
WHEN MY MIND WANDERED, I THOUGHT OF ZUALA.
WAS SHE ALIVE LIKE I WAS? OR WAS SHE ALREADY DEAD?
AND WHY DID I CARE SO MUCH IF SHE WAS?

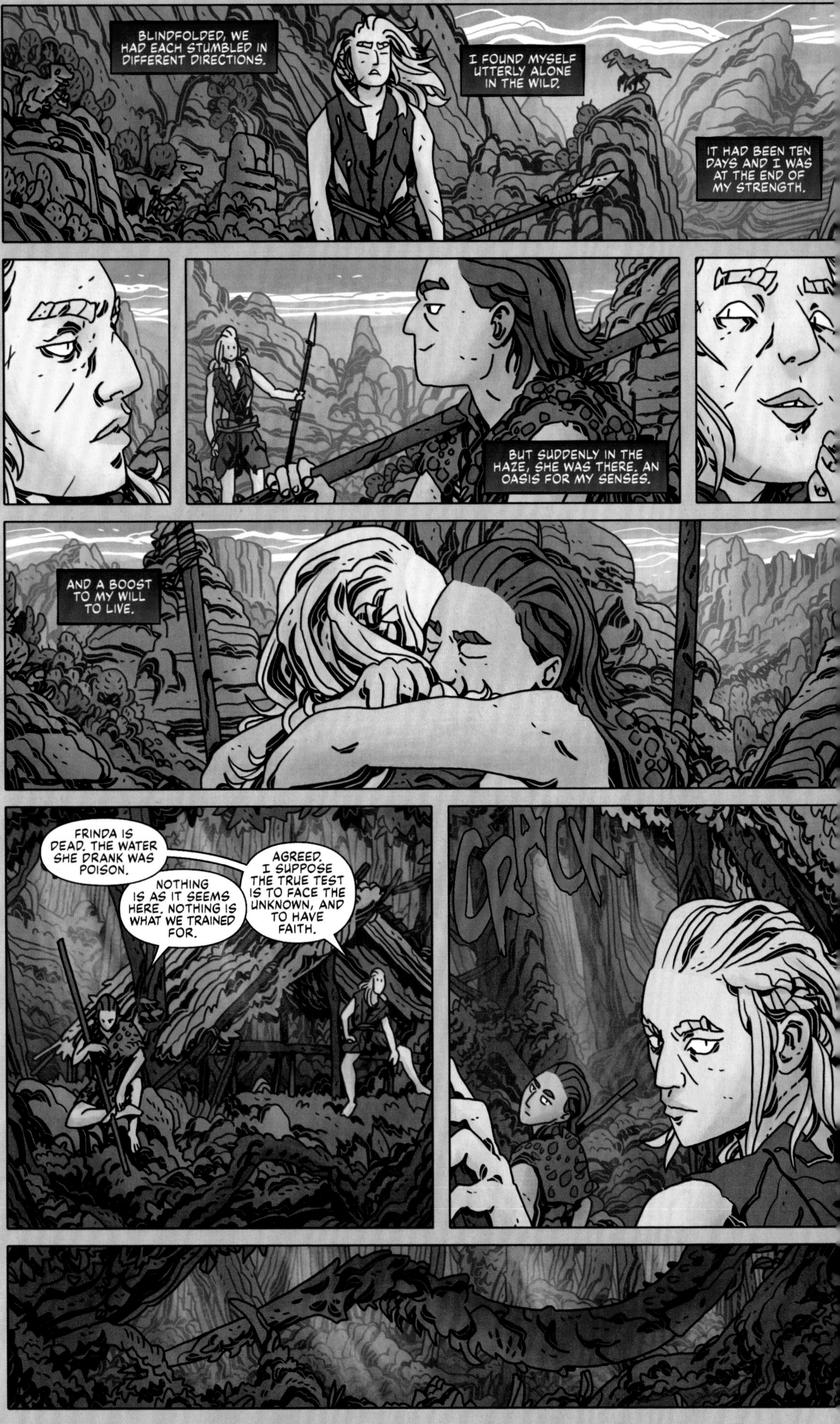
BLINDFOLDED, WE HAD EACH STUMBLED IN DIFFERENT DIRECTIONS.
I FOUND MYSELF UTTERLY ALONE IN THE WILD.
IT HAD BEEN TEN DAYS AND I WAS AT THE END OF MY STRENGTH.
BUT SUDDENLY IN THE HAZE, SHE WAS THERE. AN OASIS FOR MY SENSES.
AND A BOOST TO MY WILL TO LIVE.
FRINDA IS DEAD. THE WATER SHE DRANK WAS POISON.
NOTHING IS AS IT SEEMS HERE. NOTHING IS WHAT WE TRAINED FOR.
AGREED. I SUPPOSE THE TRUE TEST IS TO FACE THE UNKNOWN, AND TO HAVE FAITH.
CRACK

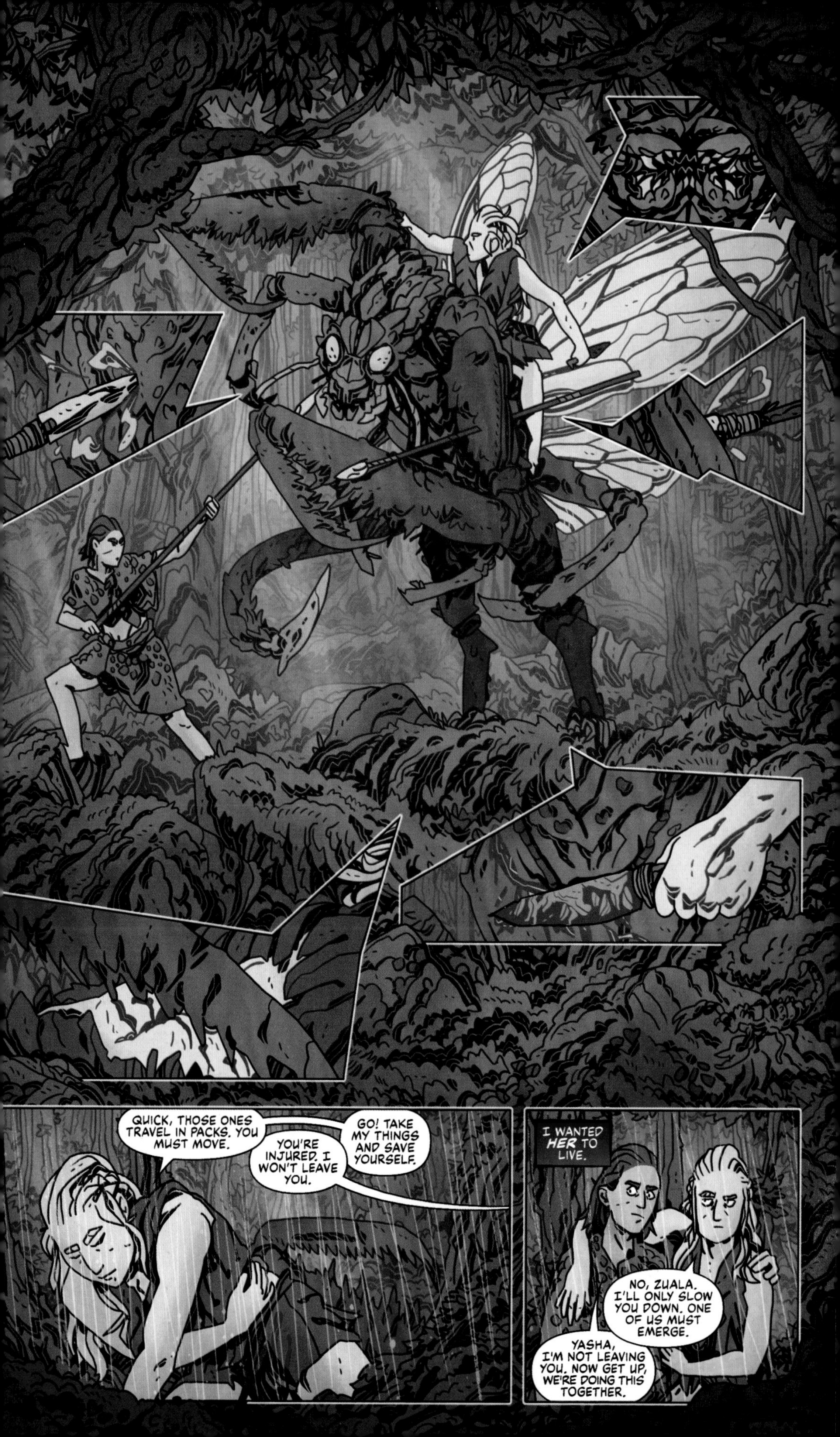
QUICK, THOSE ONES TRAVEL IN PACKS. YOU MUST MOVE.
YOU'RE INJURED. I WON'T LEAVE YOU.
GO! TAKE MY THINGS AND SAVE YOURSELF.
I WANTED HER TO LIVE.
NO, ZUALA. I'LL ONLY SLOW YOU DOWN. ONE OF US MUST EMERGE.
YASHA, I'M NOT LEAVING YOU. NOW GET UP, WE'RE DOING THIS TOGETHER.

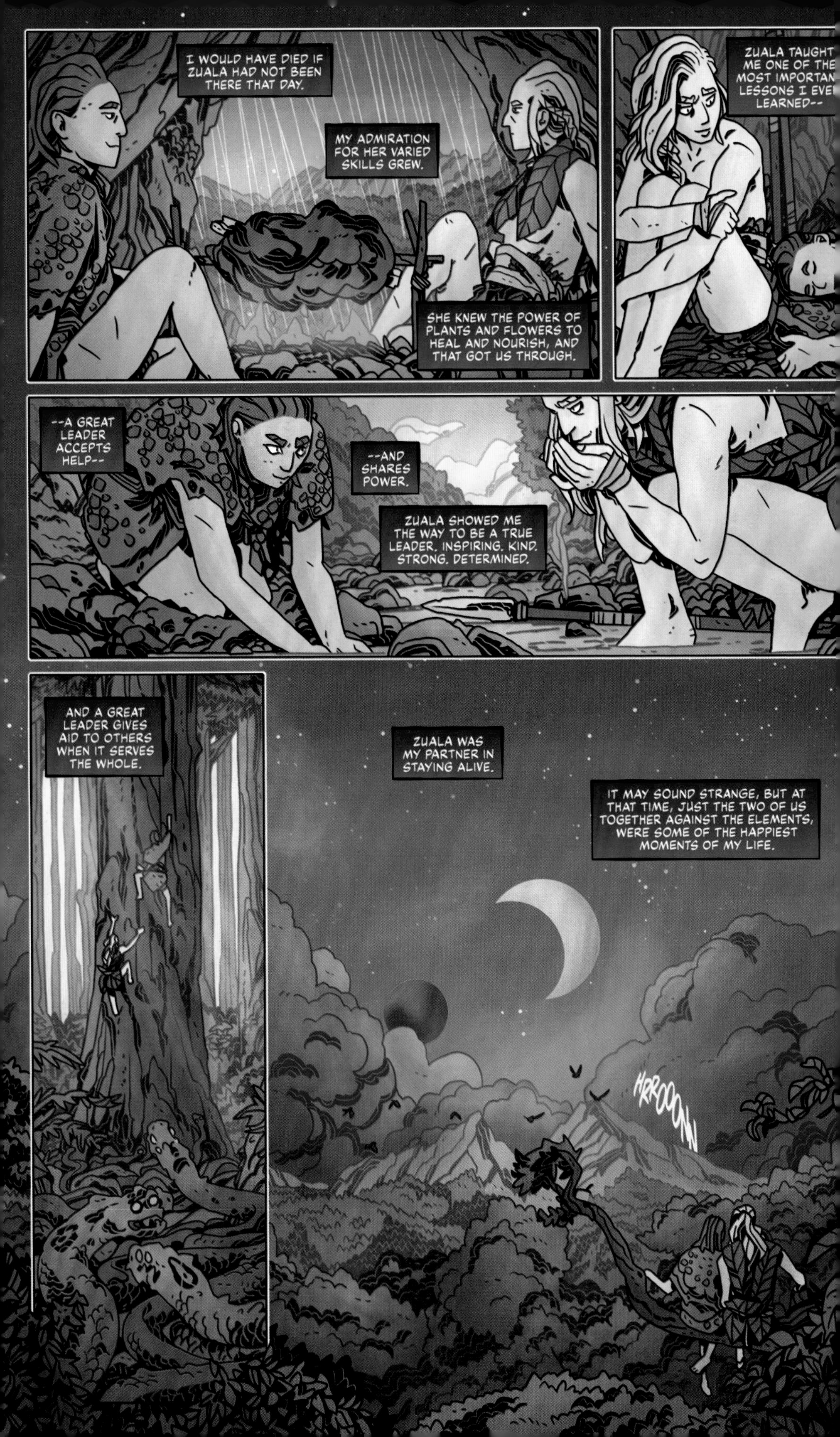
I WOULD HAVE DIED IF ZUALA HAD NOT BEEN THERE THAT DAY.
MY ADMIRATION FOR HER VARIED SKILLS GREW.
SHE KNEW THE POWER OF PLANTS AND FLOWERS TO HEAL AND NOURISH, AND THAT GOT US THROUGH.
ZUALA TAUGHT ME ONE OF THE MOST IMPORTAN LESSONS I EVE LEARNED--
--A GREAT LEADER ACCEPTS HELP--
--AND SHARES POWER.
ZUALA SHOWED ME THE WAY TO BE A TRUE LEADER. INSPIRING. KIND. STRONG. DETERMINED.
AND A GREAT LEADER GIVES AID TO OTHERS WHEN IT SERVES THE WHOLE.
ZUALA WAS MY PARTNER IN STAYING ALIVE.
IT MAY SOUND STRANGE, BUT AT THAT TIME, JUST THE TWO OF US TOGETHER AGAINST THE ELEMENTS, WERE SOME OF THE HAPPIEST MOMENTS OF MY LIFE.
HRROOONN

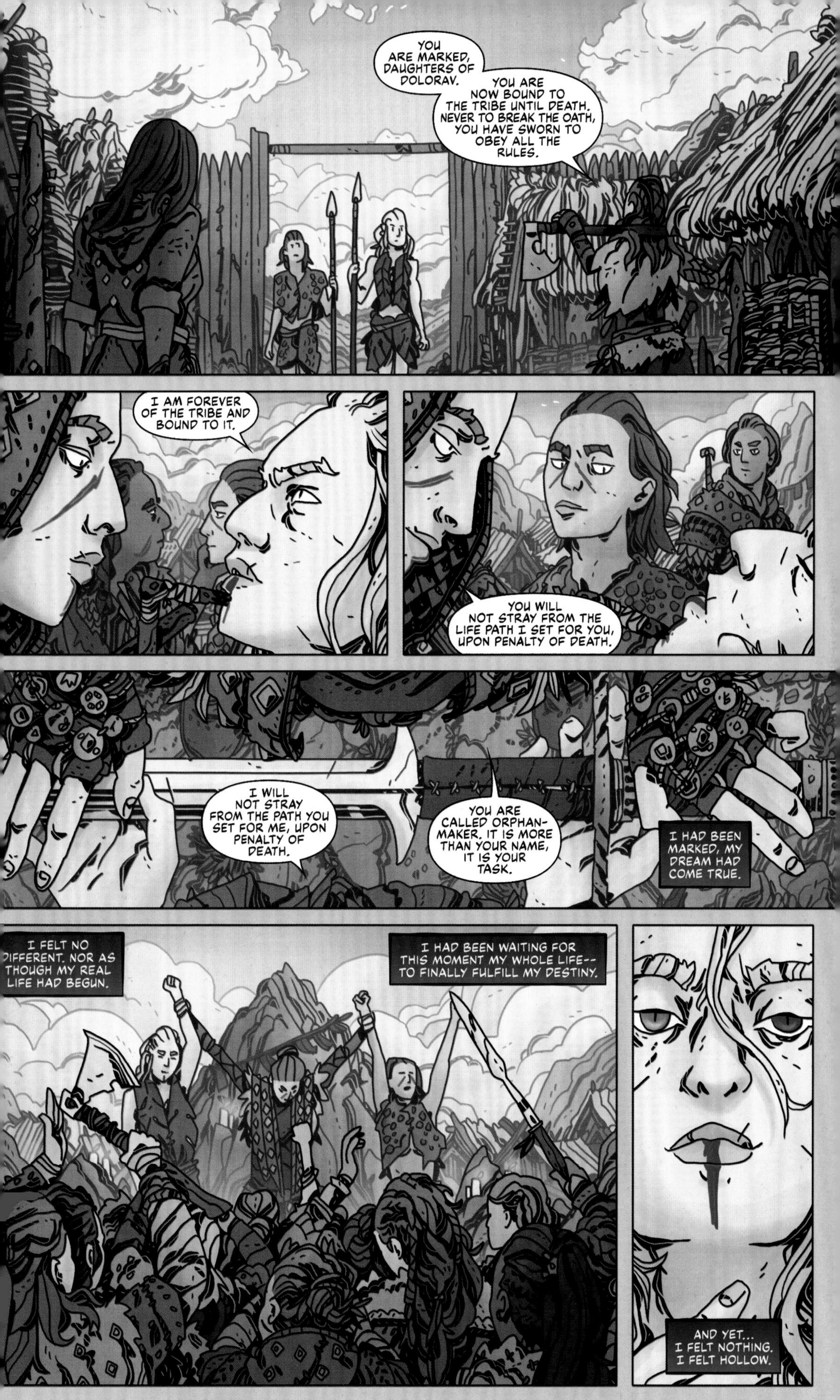
YOU ARE MARKED, DAUGHTERS OF DOLORAV.
YOU ARE NOW BOUND TO THE TRIBE UNTIL DEATH. NEVER TO BREAK THE OATH, YOU HAVE SWORN TO OBEY ALL THE RULES.
I AM FOREVER OF THE TRIBE AND BOUND TO IT.
YOU WILL NOT STRAY FROM THE LIFE PATH I SET FOR YOU, UPON PENALTY OF DEATH.
I WILL NOT STRAY FROM THE PATH YOU SET FOR ME, UPON PENALTY OF DEATH.
YOU ARE CALLED ORPHAN-MAKER. IT IS MORE THAN YOUR NAME, IT IS YOUR TASK.
I HAD BEEN MARKED, MY DREAM HAD COME TRUE.
I FELT NO DIFFERENT. NOR AS THOUGH MY REAL LIFE HAD BEGUN.
I HAD BEEN WAITING FOR THIS MOMENT MY WHOLE LIFE-- TO FINALLY FULFILL MY DESTINY.
AND YET... I FELT NOTHING. I FELT HOLLOW.

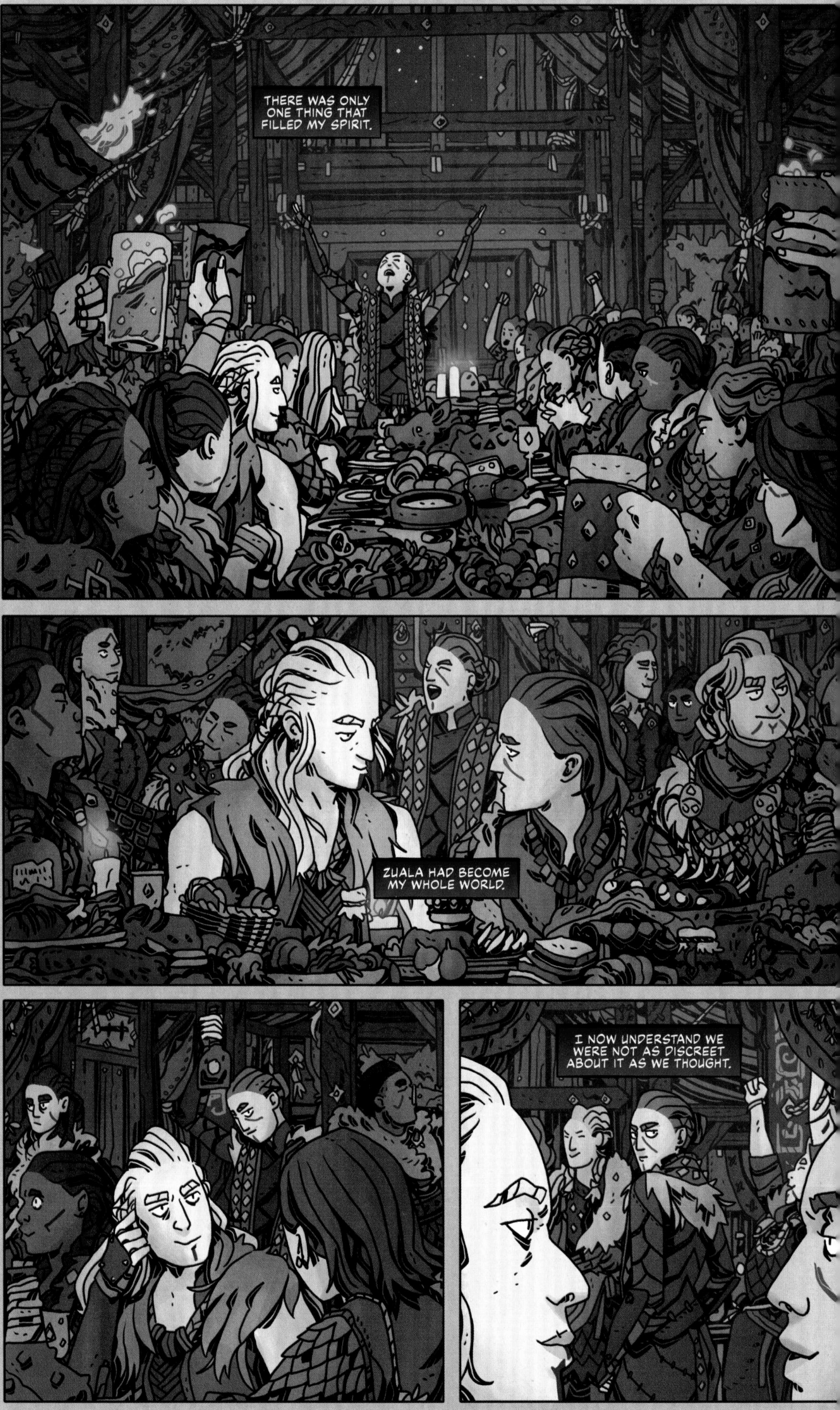
THERE WAS ONLY ONE THING THAT FILLED MY SPIRIT.
ZUALA HAD BECOME MY WHOLE WORLD.
I NOW UNDERSTAND WE WERE NOT AS DISCREET ABOUT IT AS WE THOUGHT.

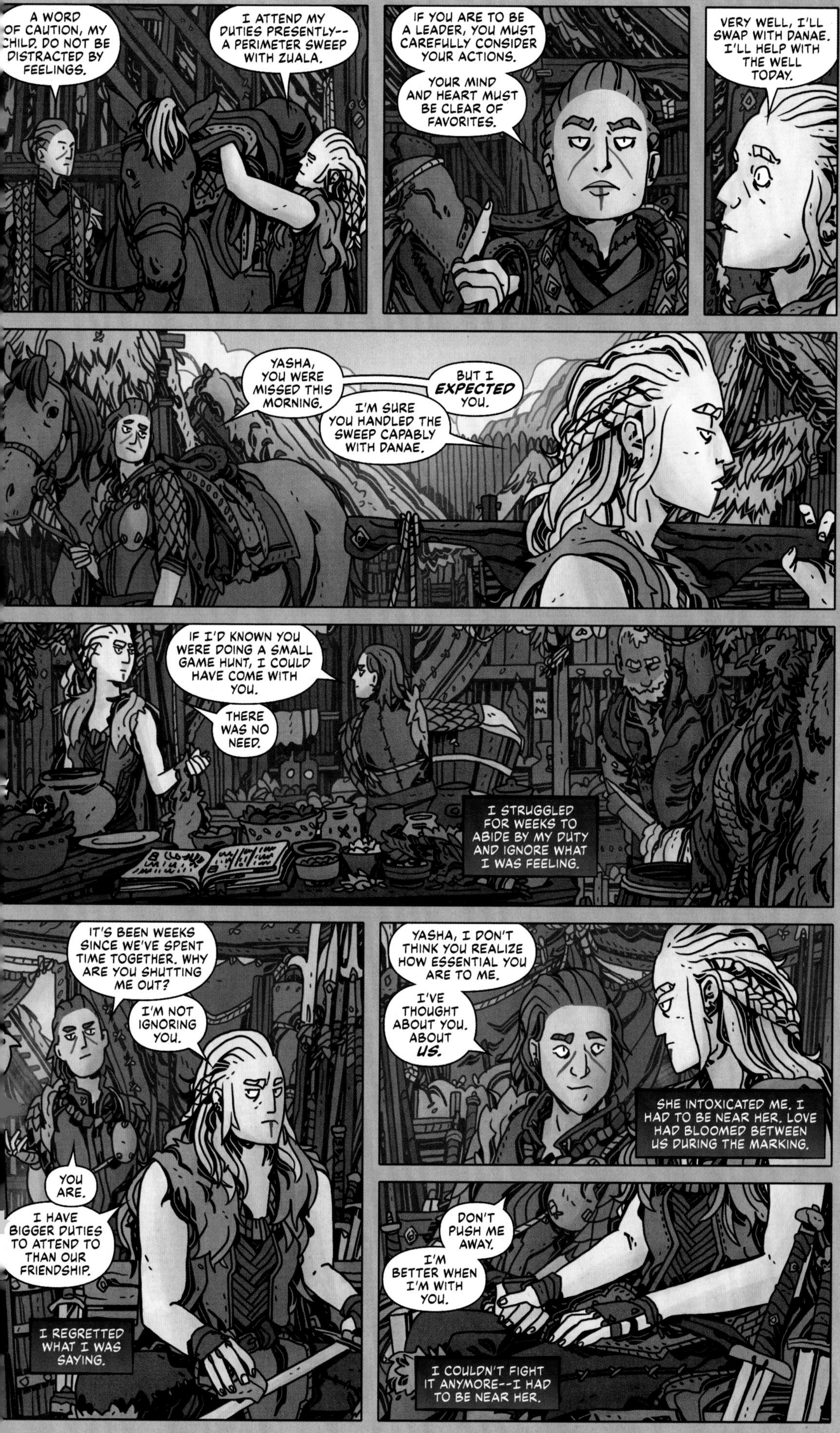
A WORD OF CAUTION, MY CHILD. DO NOT BE DISTRACTED BY FEELINGS.
I ATTEND MY DUTIES PRESENTLY-- A PERIMETER SWEEP WITH ZUALA.
IF YOU ARE TO BE A LEADER, YOU MUST CAREFULLY CONSIDER YOUR ACTIONS.
YOUR MIND AND HEART MUST BE CLEAR OF FAVORITES.
VERY WELL, I'LL SWAP WITH DANAE. I'LL HELP WITH THE WELL TODAY.
YASHA, YOU WERE MISSED THIS MORNING.
BUT I *EXPECTED* YOU.
I'M SURE YOU HANDLED THE SWEEP CAPABLY WITH DANAE.
IF I'D KNOWN YOU WERE DOING A SMALL GAME HUNT, I COULD HAVE COME WITH YOU.
THERE WAS NO NEED.
I STRUGGLED FOR WEEKS TO ABIDE BY MY DUTY AND IGNORE WHAT I WAS FEELING.
IT'S BEEN WEEKS SINCE WE'VE SPENT TIME TOGETHER. WHY ARE YOU SHUTTING ME OUT?
I'M NOT IGNORING YOU.
YOU ARE.
I HAVE BIGGER DUTIES TO ATTEND TO THAN OUR FRIENDSHIP.
I REGRETTED WHAT I WAS SAYING.
YASHA, I DON'T THINK YOU REALIZE HOW ESSENTIAL YOU ARE TO ME.
I'VE THOUGHT ABOUT YOU. ABOUT *US.*
SHE INTOXICATED ME. I HAD TO BE NEAR HER. LOVE HAD BLOOMED BETWEEN US DURING THE MARKING.
DON'T PUSH ME AWAY.
I'M BETTER WHEN I'M WITH YOU.
I COULDN'T FIGHT IT ANYMORE--I HAD TO BE NEAR HER.

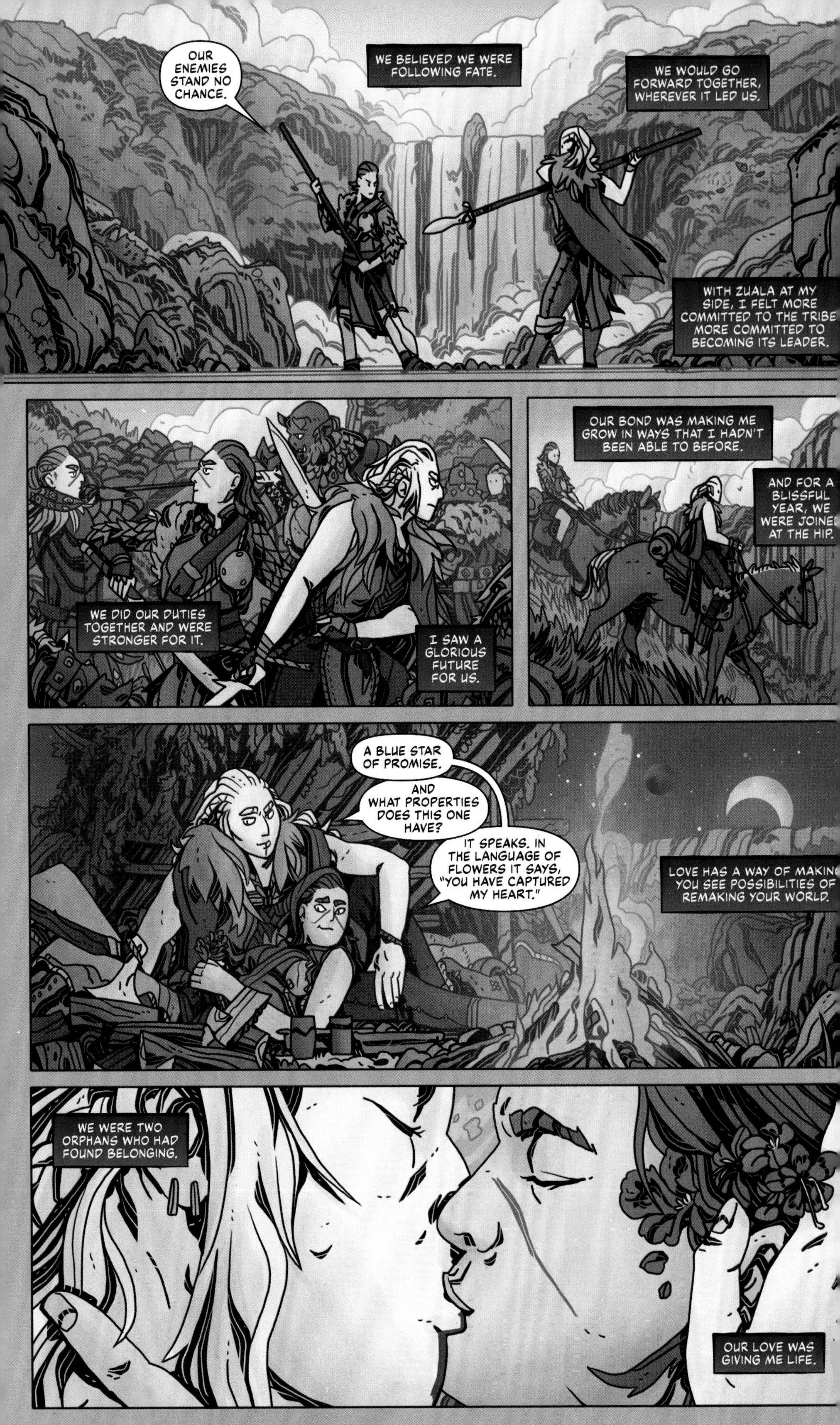
OUR ENEMIES STAND NO CHANCE.
WE BELIEVED WE WERE FOLLOWING FATE.
WE WOULD GO FORWARD TOGETHER, WHEREVER IT LED US.
WITH ZUALA AT MY SIDE, I FELT MORE COMMITTED TO THE TRIBE MORE COMMITTED TO BECOMING ITS LEADER.
WE DID OUR DUTIES TOGETHER AND WERE STRONGER FOR IT.
I SAW A GLORIOUS FUTURE FOR US.
OUR BOND WAS MAKING ME GROW IN WAYS THAT I HADN'T BEEN ABLE TO BEFORE.
AND FOR A BLISSFUL YEAR, WE WERE JOINE AT THE HIP.
A BLUE STAR OF PROMISE.
AND WHAT PROPERTIES DOES THIS ONE HAVE?
IT SPEAKS. IN THE LANGUAGE OF FLOWERS IT SAYS, "YOU HAVE CAPTURED MY HEART."
LOVE HAS A WAY OF MAKIN YOU SEE POSSIBILITIES OF REMAKING YOUR WORLD.
WE WERE TWO ORPHANS WHO HAD FOUND BELONGING.
OUR LOVE WAS GIVING ME LIFE.

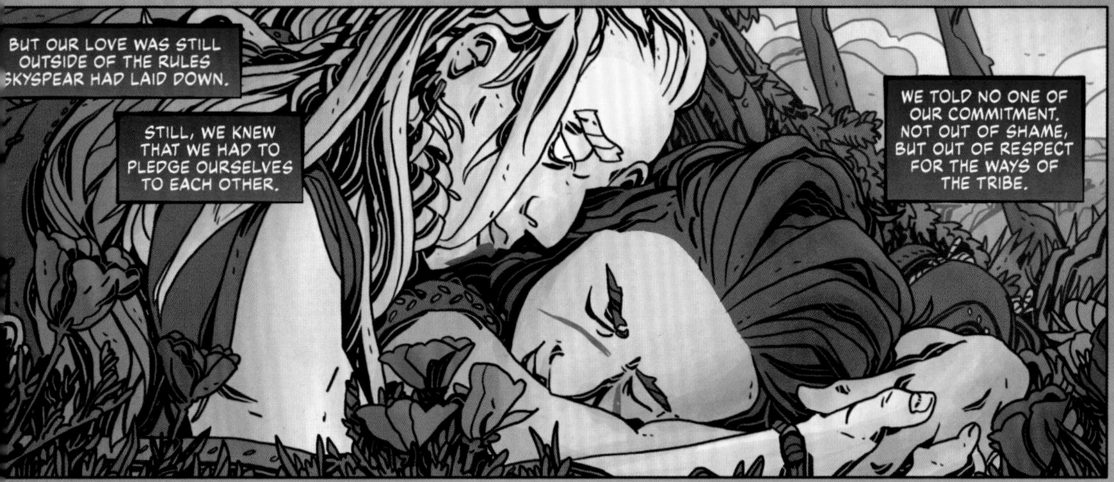
BUT OUR LOVE WAS STILL OUTSIDE OF THE RULES SKYSPEAR HAD LAID DOWN.
STILL, WE KNEW THAT WE HAD TO PLEDGE OURSELVES TO EACH OTHER.
WE TOLD NO ONE OF OUR COMMITMENT. NOT OUT OF SHAME, BUT OUT OF RESPECT FOR THE WAYS OF THE TRIBE.

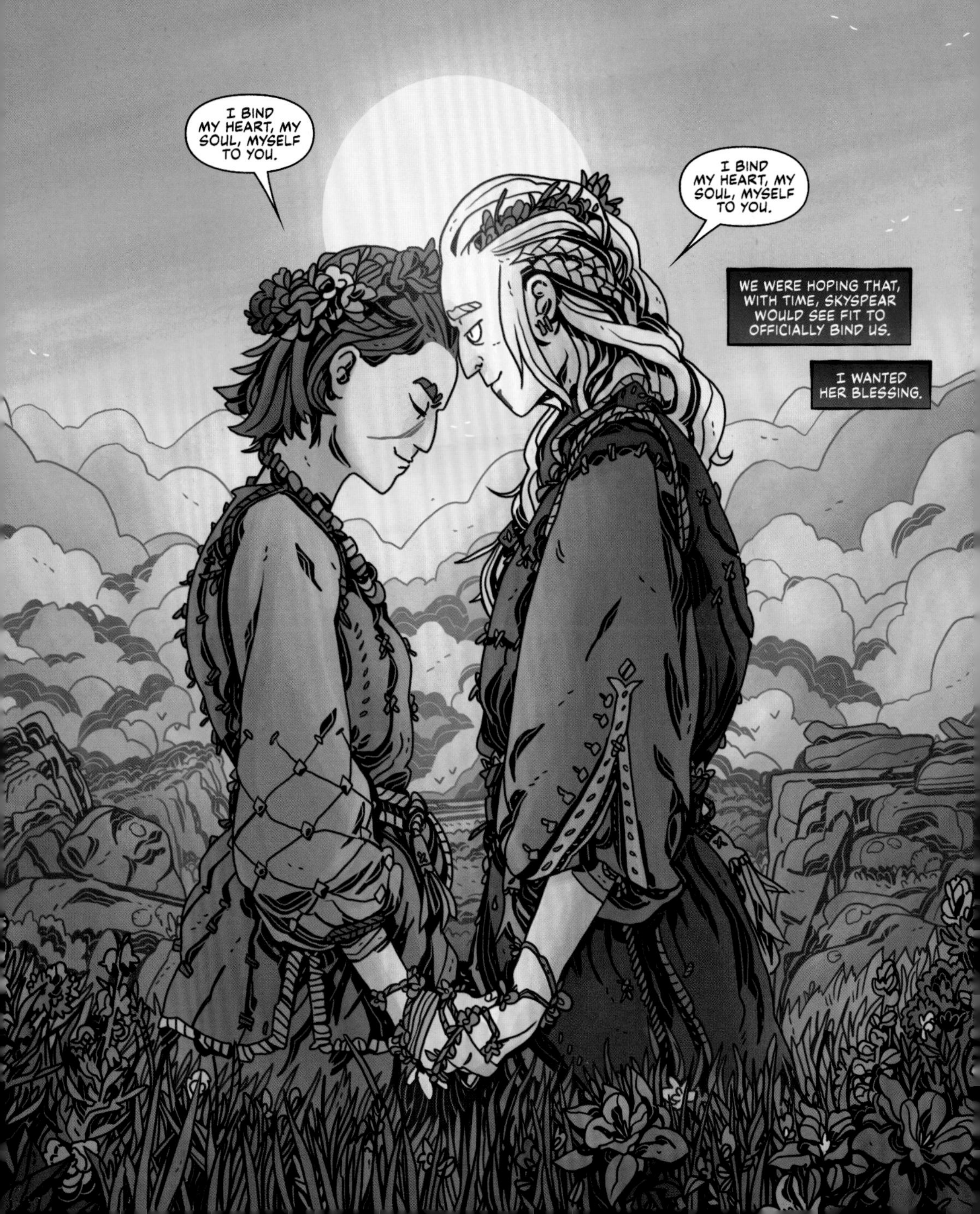
I BIND MY HEART, MY SOUL, MYSELF TO YOU.
I BIND MY HEART, MY SOUL, MYSELF TO YOU.
WE WERE HOPING THAT, WITH TIME, SKYSPEAR WOULD SEE FIT TO OFFICIALLY BIND US.
I WANTED HER BLESSING.

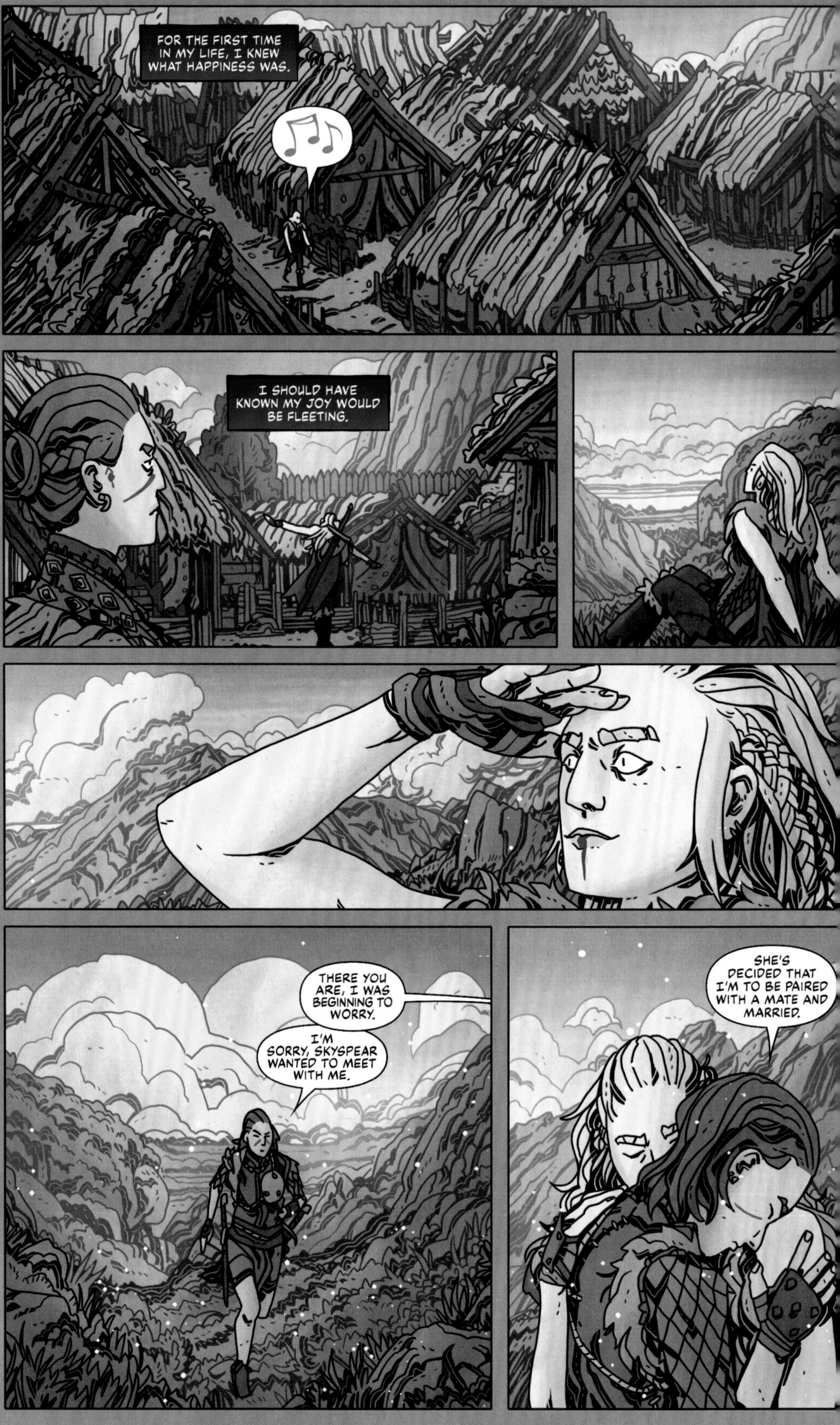
FOR THE FIRST TIME IN MY LIFE, I KNEW WHAT HAPPINESS WAS.
I SHOULD HAVE KNOWN MY JOY WOULD BE FLEETING.
THERE YOU ARE, I WAS BEGINNING TO WORRY.
I'M SORRY, SKYSPEAR WANTED TO MEET WITH ME.
SHE'S DECIDED THAT I'M TO BE PAIRED WITH A MATE AND MARRIED.

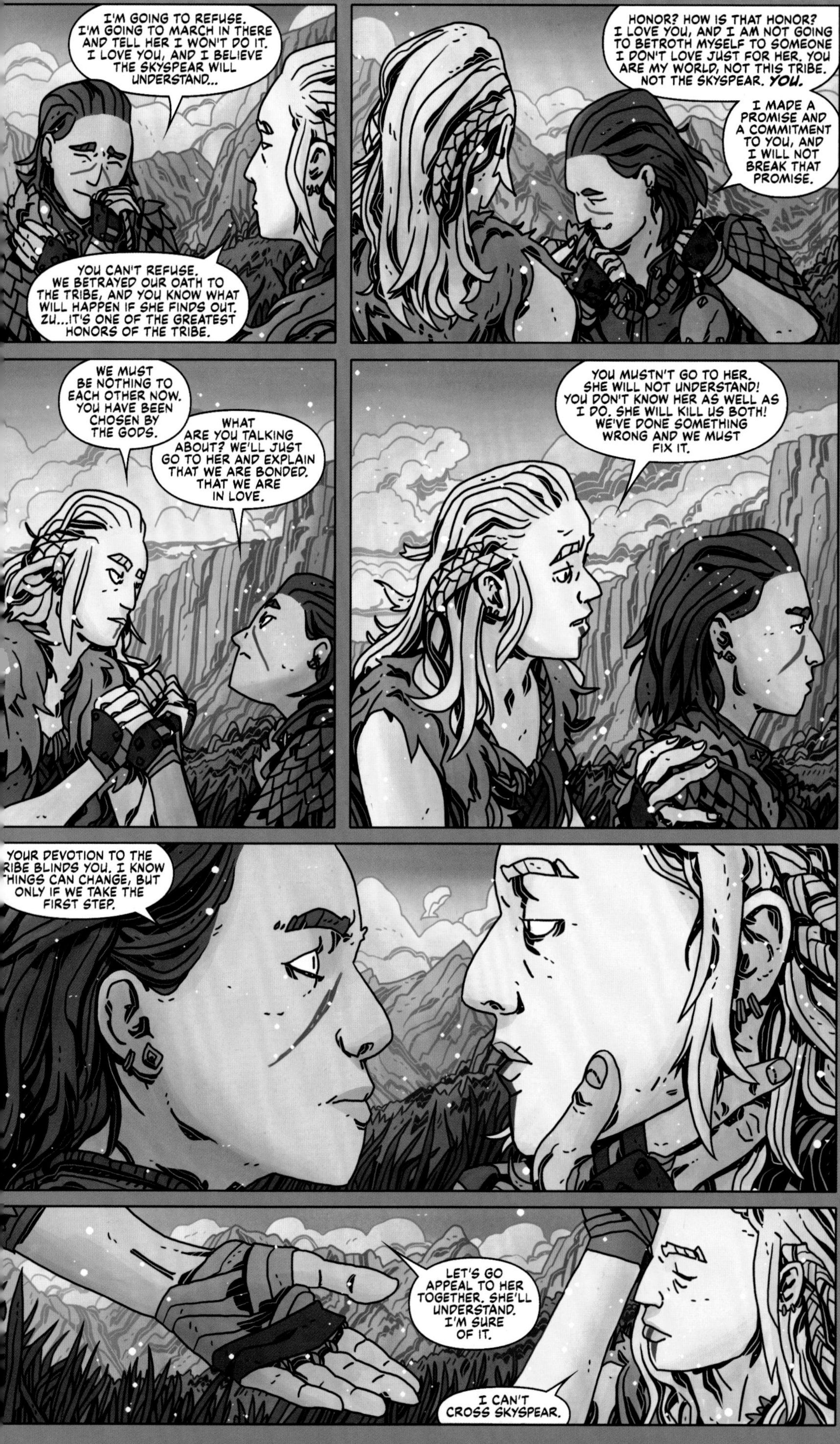
I'M GOING TO REFUSE. I'M GOING TO MARCH IN THERE AND TELL HER I WON'T DO IT. I LOVE YOU, AND I BELIEVE THE SKYSPEAR WILL UNDERSTAND...
YOU CAN'T REFUSE. WE BETRAYED OUR OATH TO THE TRIBE, AND YOU KNOW WHAT WILL HAPPEN IF SHE FINDS OUT. ZU...IT'S ONE OF THE GREATEST HONORS OF THE TRIBE.
HONOR? HOW IS THAT HONOR? I LOVE YOU, AND I AM NOT GOING TO BETROTH MYSELF TO SOMEONE I DON'T LOVE JUST FOR HER. YOU ARE MY WORLD, NOT THIS TRIBE. NOT THE SKYSPEAR. *YOU.*
I MADE A PROMISE AND A COMMITMENT TO YOU, AND I WILL NOT BREAK THAT PROMISE.
WE MUST BE NOTHING TO EACH OTHER NOW. YOU HAVE BEEN CHOSEN BY THE GODS.
WHAT ARE YOU TALKING ABOUT? WE'LL JUST GO TO HER AND EXPLAIN THAT WE ARE BONDED. THAT WE ARE IN LOVE.
YOU MUSTN'T GO TO HER. SHE WILL NOT UNDERSTAND! YOU DON'T KNOW HER AS WELL AS I DO. SHE WILL KILL US BOTH! WE'VE DONE SOMETHING WRONG AND WE MUST FIX IT.
YOUR DEVOTION TO THE TRIBE BLINDS YOU. I KNOW THINGS CAN CHANGE, BUT ONLY IF WE TAKE THE FIRST STEP.
LET'S GO APPEAL TO HER TOGETHER. SHE'LL UNDERSTAND. I'M SURE OF IT.
I CAN'T CROSS SKYSPEAR.

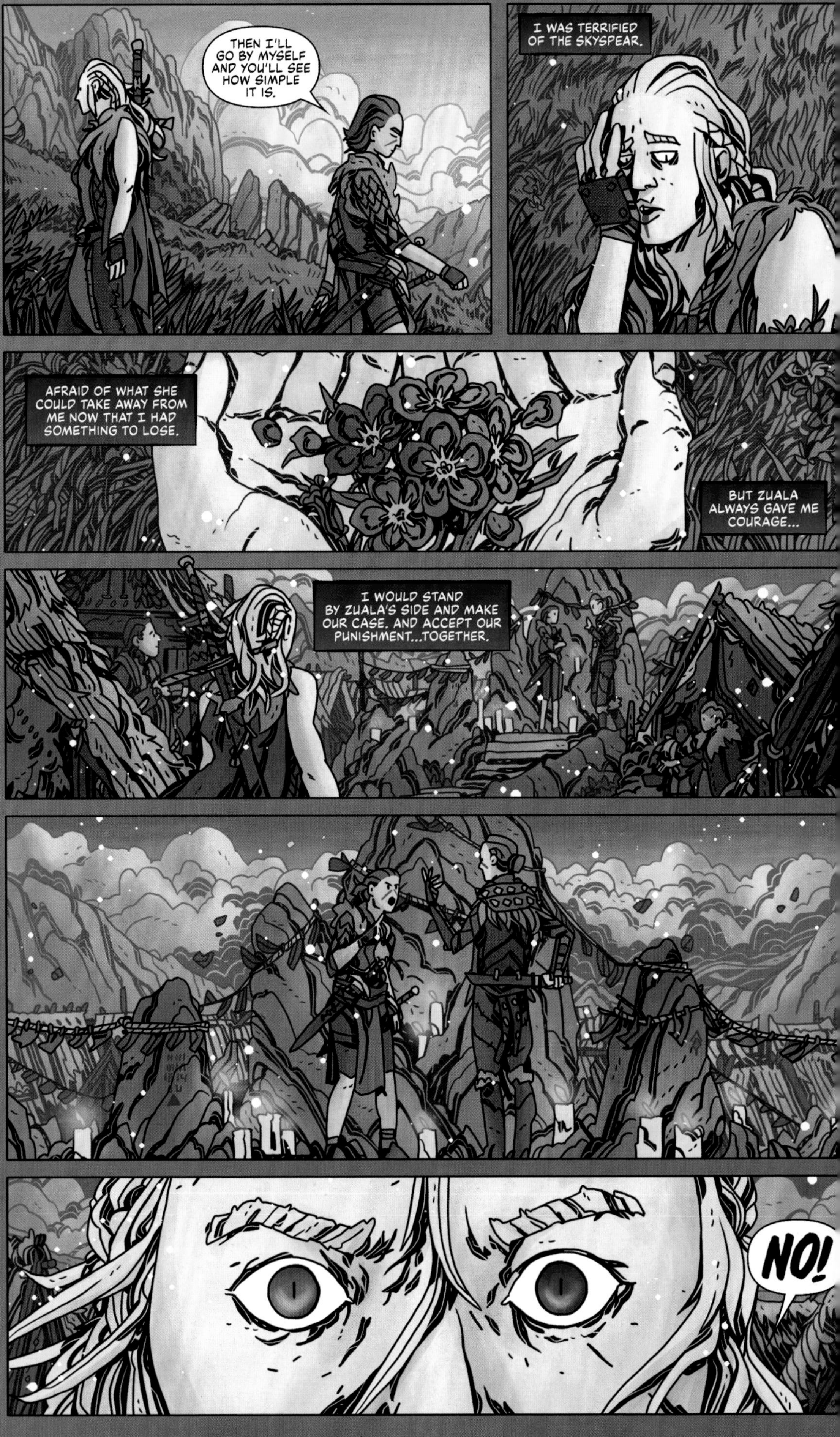
THEN I'LL GO BY MYSELF AND YOU'LL SEE HOW SIMPLE IT IS.
I WAS TERRIFIED OF THE SKYSPEAR.
AFRAID OF WHAT SHE COULD TAKE AWAY FROM ME NOW THAT I HAD SOMETHING TO LOSE.
BUT ZUALA ALWAYS GAVE ME COURAGE...
I WOULD STAND BY ZUALA'S SIDE AND MAKE OUR CASE. AND ACCEPT OUR PUNISHMENT...TOGETHER.
NO!

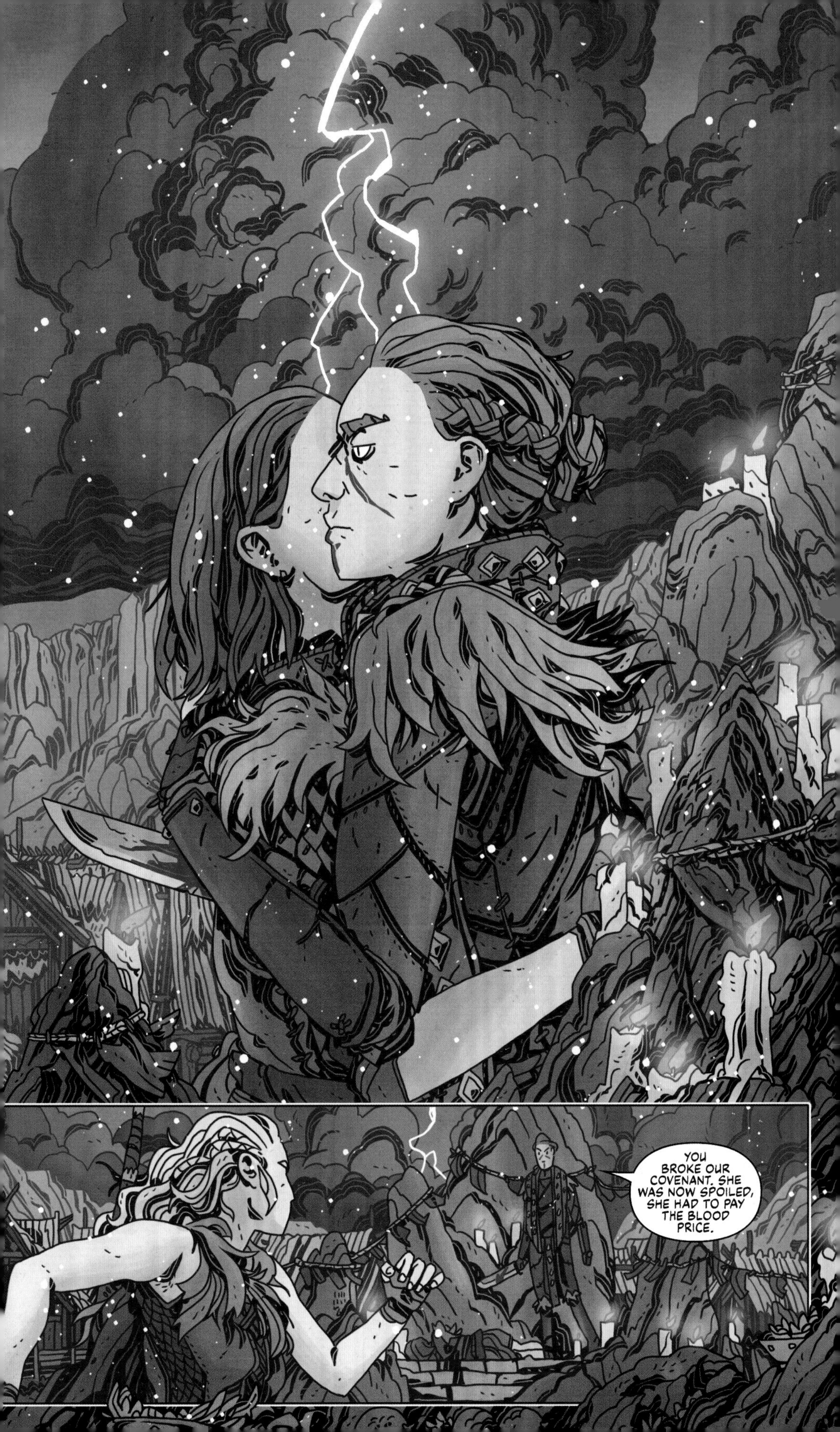
YOU BROKE OUR COVENANT. SHE WAS NOW SPOILED, SHE HAD TO PAY THE BLOOD PRICE.

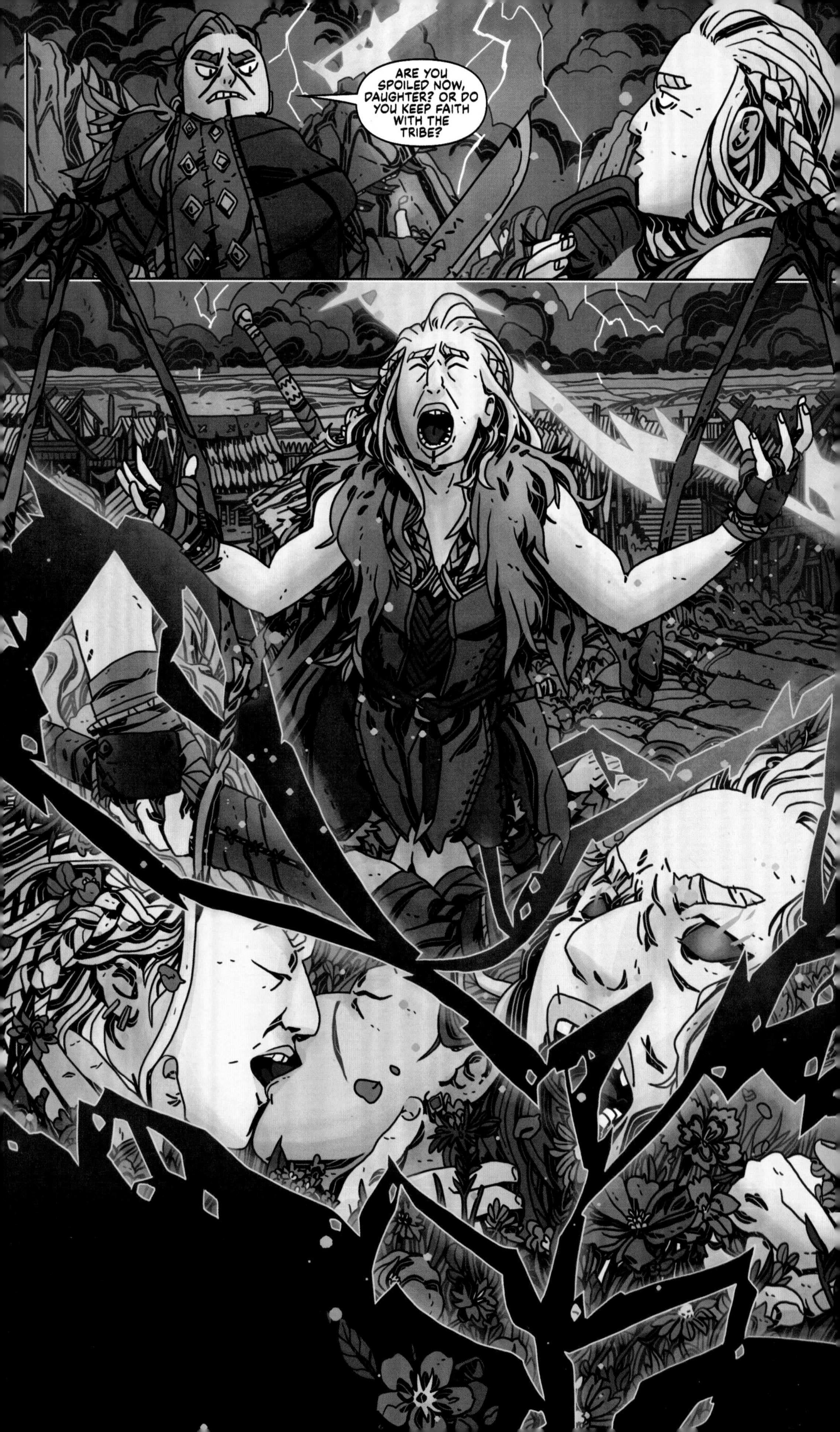
ARE YOU SPOILED NOW, DAUGHTER? OR DO YOU KEEP FAITH WITH THE TRIBE?

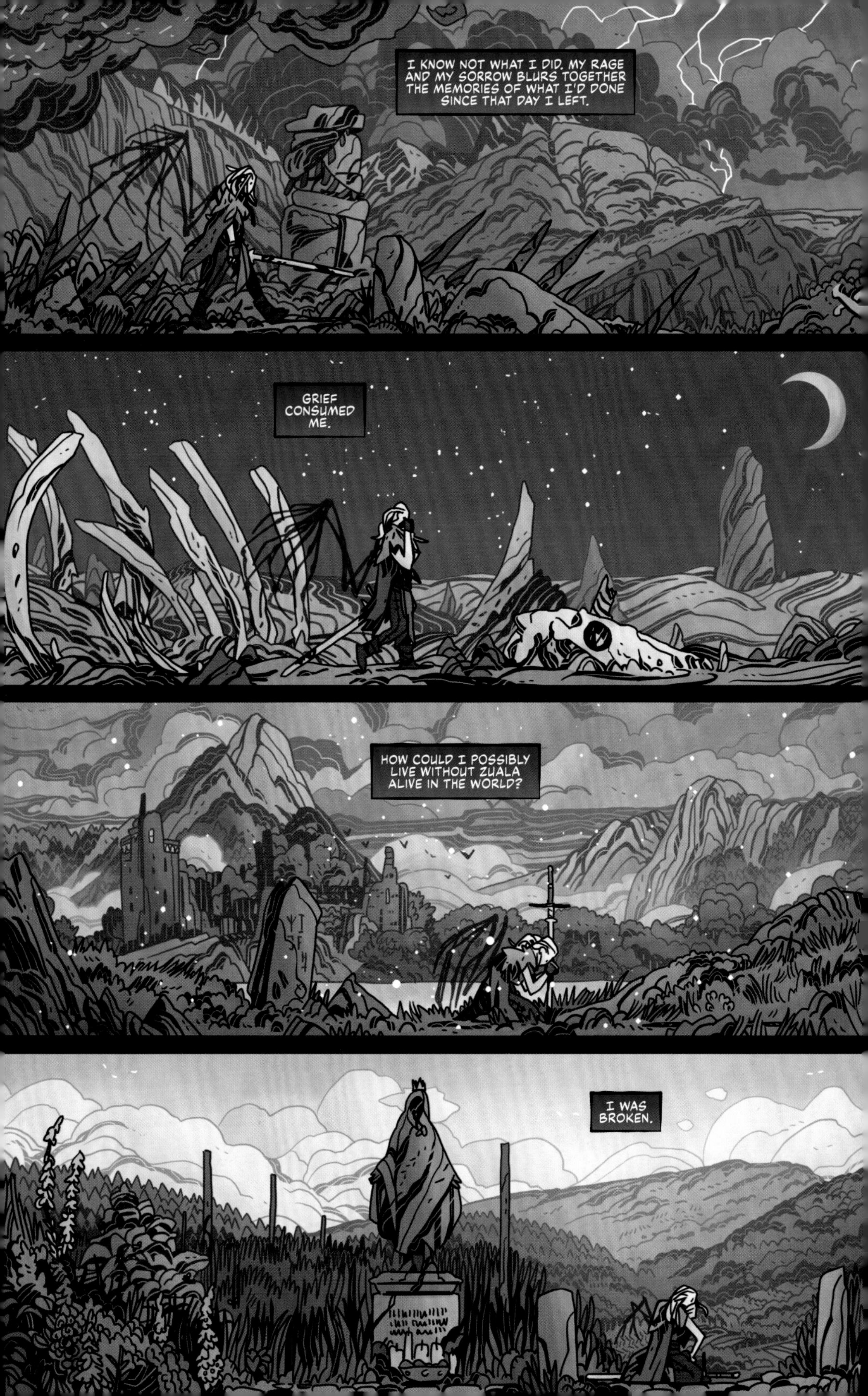
I KNOW NOT WHAT I DID. MY RAGE AND MY SORROW BLURS TOGETHER THE MEMORIES OF WHAT I'D DONE SINCE THAT DAY I LEFT.
GRIEF CONSUMED ME.
HOW COULD I POSSIBLY LIVE WITHOUT ZUALA ALIVE IN THE WORLD?
I WAS BROKEN.

I GREW UP KNOWING NOTHING OF THE LARGER WORLD EXCEPT THAT WHAT IT HAD TO OFFER WAS POISON.

I HAD BEEN TAUGHT TO BE SUSPICIOUS OF IT, TO AVOID IT.

IS THAT ALL YOU'VE GOT? DON'T GO EASY ON ME...

BUT NOW I WOULD EMBRACE THE POISON THE OUTSIDE OFFERED...

...AS I SOUGHT AN EXIT FROM MY UNBEARABLE PAIN.

YOU'LL REGRET BOTHERING ME.

SHOW ME HOW MUCH I'LL REGRET IT.

I WAS RECKLESS. I WAS CARELESS.

I THOUGHT I DESERVED EVERY ACHE, EVERY HURT.

OI. OI. I DON'T WANT TO SEE YOUR FACE IN HERE AGAIN.

WE'LL HAVE NONE OF THAT HERE.

EVERY THOUGHT LED TO ZUALA. I YEARNED TO HOLD HER IN MY ARMS AGAIN.

THE PAIN SHARPENED WHE I REMEMBERED I'D ALSO LOST MY WHOLE WORLD, MY WHOLE WAY OF LIFE.

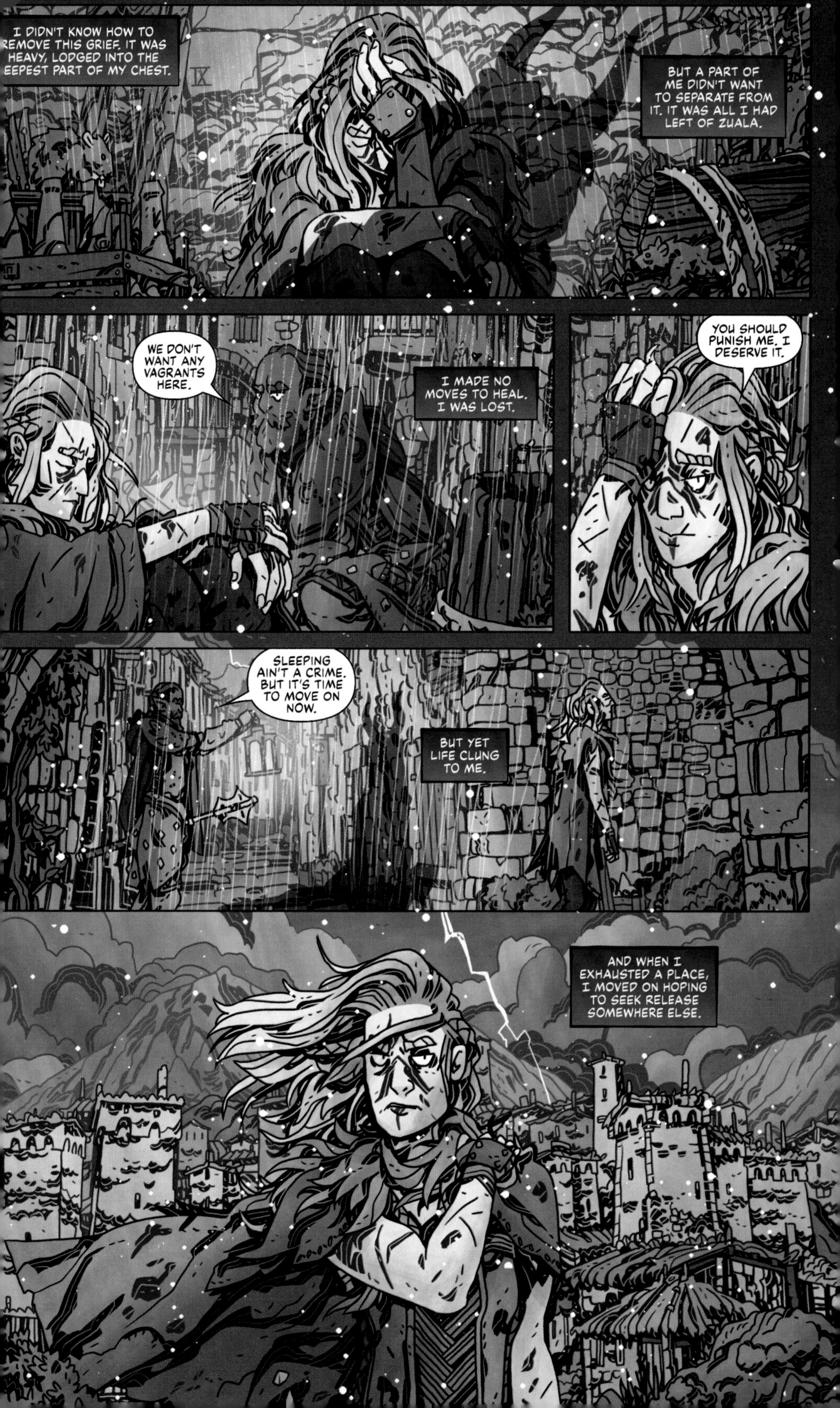

I DIDN'T KNOW HOW TO REMOVE THIS GRIEF. IT WAS HEAVY, LODGED INTO THE EEPEST PART OF MY CHEST.
BUT A PART OF ME DIDN'T WANT TO SEPARATE FROM IT. IT WAS ALL I HAD LEFT OF ZUALA.
WE DON'T WANT ANY VAGRANTS HERE.
I MADE NO MOVES TO HEAL. I WAS LOST.
YOU SHOULD PUNISH ME. I DESERVE IT.
SLEEPING AIN'T A CRIME. BUT IT'S TIME TO MOVE ON NOW.
BUT YET LIFE CLUNG TO ME.
AND WHEN I EXHAUSTED A PLACE, I MOVED ON HOPING TO SEEK RELEASE SOMEWHERE ELSE.

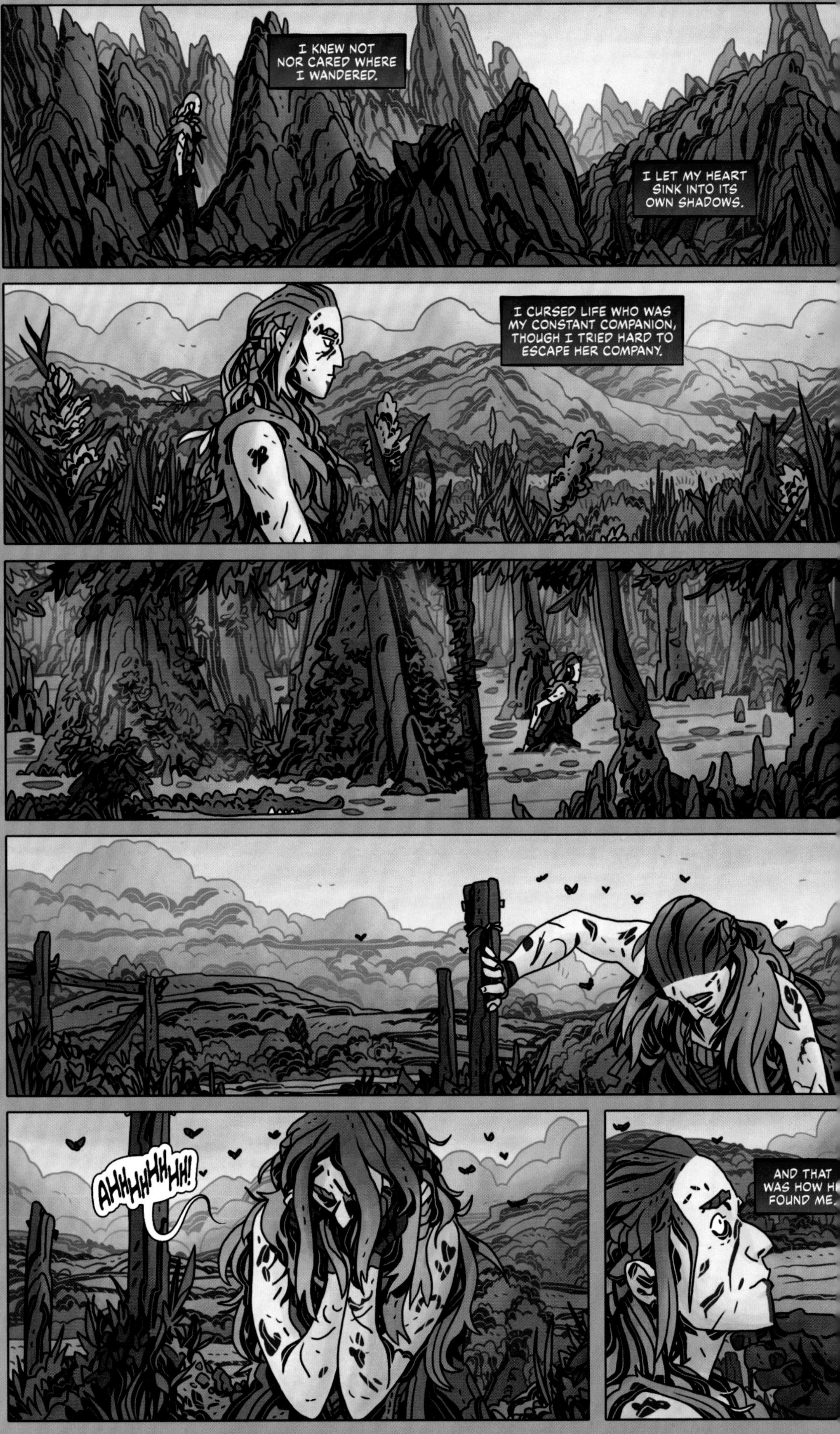
I KNEW NOT NOR CARED WHERE I WANDERED.
I LET MY HEART SINK INTO ITS OWN SHADOWS.
I CURSED LIFE WHO WAS MY CONSTANT COMPANION, THOUGH I TRIED HARD TO ESCAPE HER COMPANY.
AHHHHHHHH!
AND THAT WAS HOW H
FOUND ME.

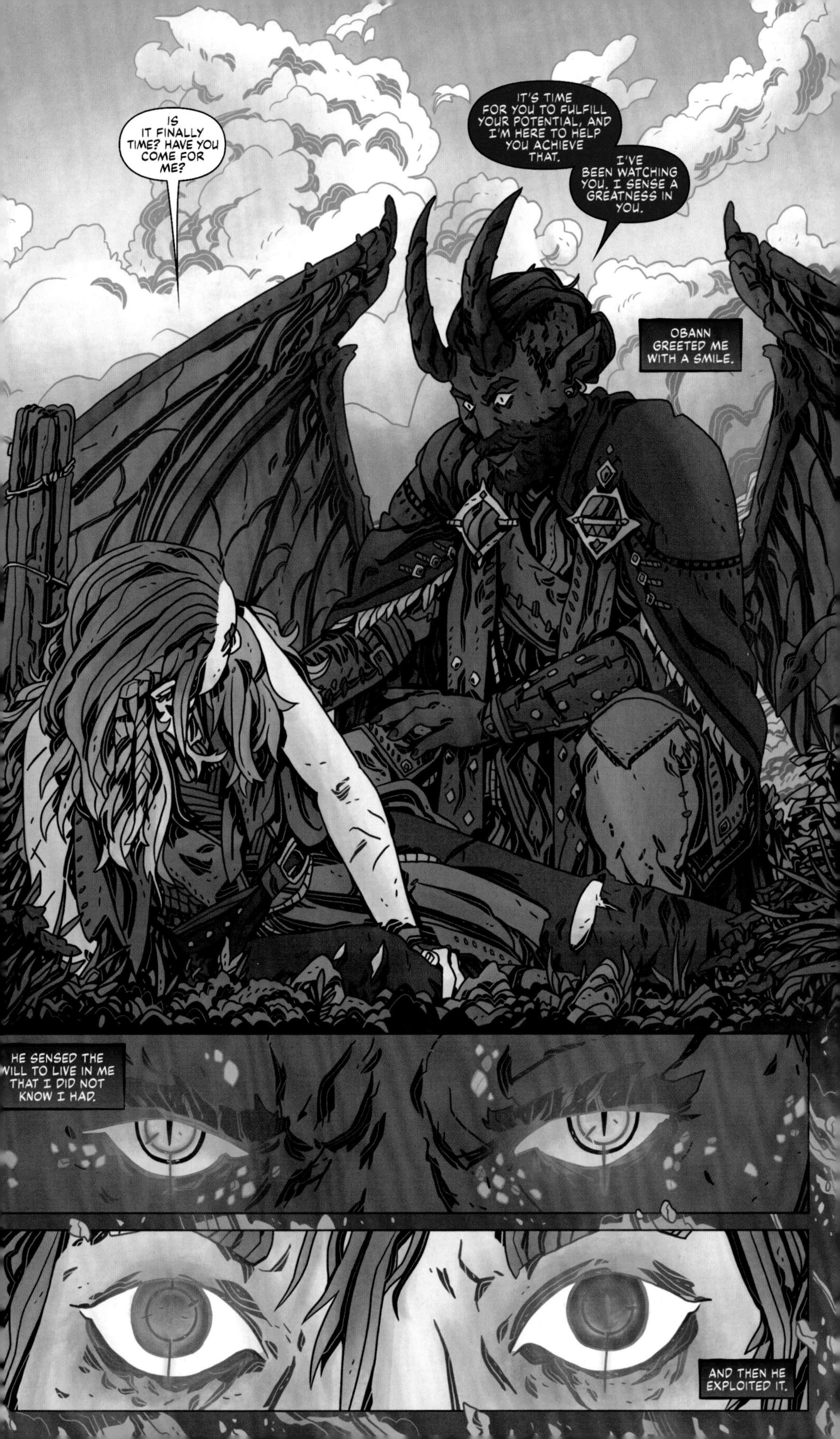
IS IT FINALLY TIME? HAVE YOU COME FOR ME?
IT'S TIME FOR YOU TO FULFILL YOUR POTENTIAL, AND I'M HERE TO HELP YOU ACHIEVE THAT.
I'VE BEEN WATCHING YOU. I SENSE A GREATNESS IN YOU.
OBANN GREETED ME WITH A SMILE.
HE SENSED THE WILL TO LIVE IN ME THAT I DID NOT KNOW I HAD.
AND THEN HE EXPLOITED IT.

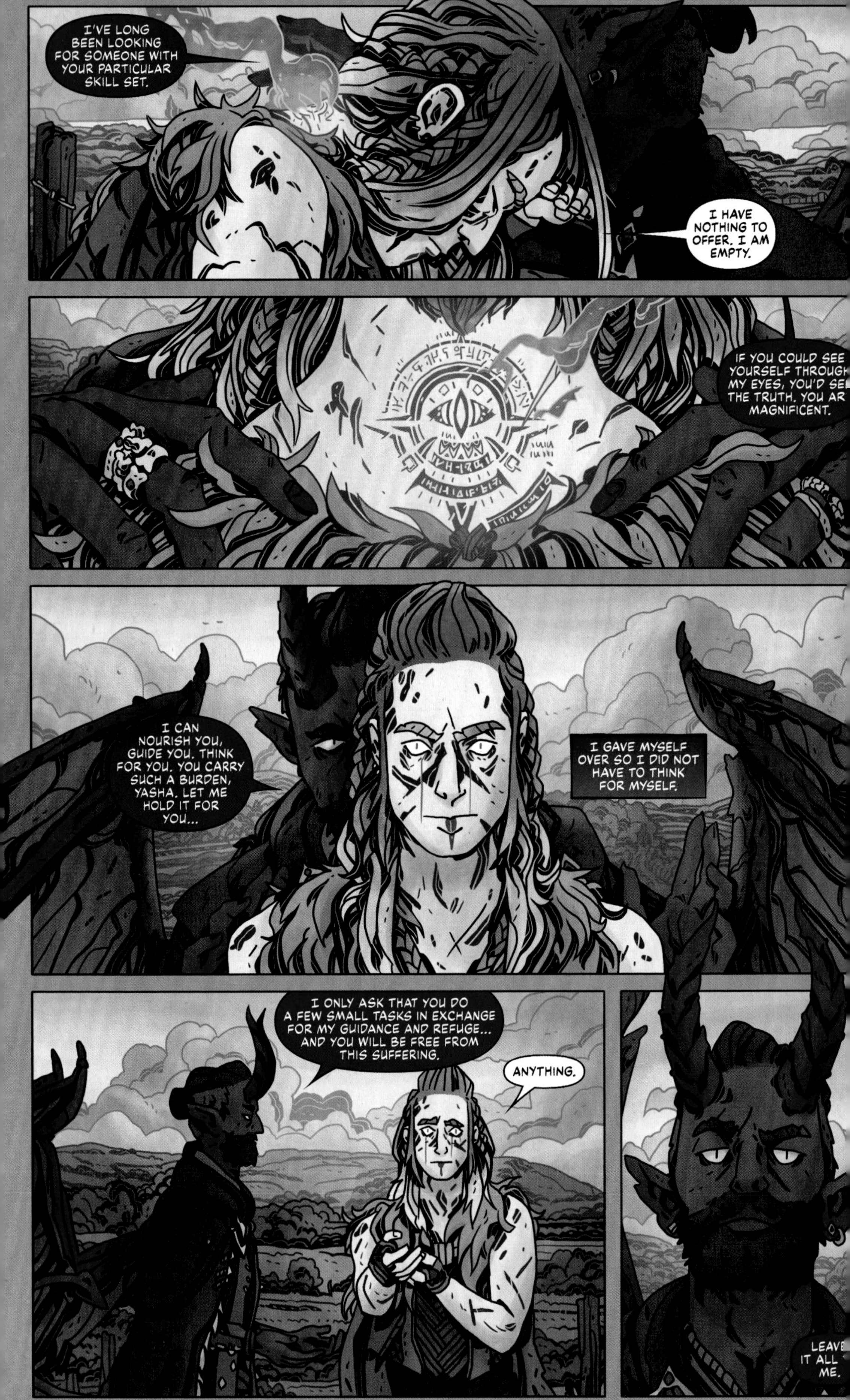
I'VE LONG BEEN LOOKING FOR SOMEONE WITH YOUR PARTICULAR SKILL SET.
I HAVE NOTHING TO OFFER. I AM EMPTY.
IF YOU COULD SEE YOURSELF THROUG MY EYES, YOU'D SE THE TRUTH. YOU AR MAGNIFICENT.
I CAN NOURISH YOU, GUIDE YOU. THINK FOR YOU. YOU CARRY SUCH A BURDEN, YASHA. LET ME HOLD IT FOR YOU...
I GAVE MYSELF OVER SO I DID NOT HAVE TO THINK FOR MYSELF.
I ONLY ASK THAT YOU DO A FEW SMALL TASKS IN EXCHANGE FOR MY GUIDANCE AND REFUGE... AND YOU WILL BE FREE FROM THIS SUFFERING.
ANYTHING.
LEAVE IT ALL ME.

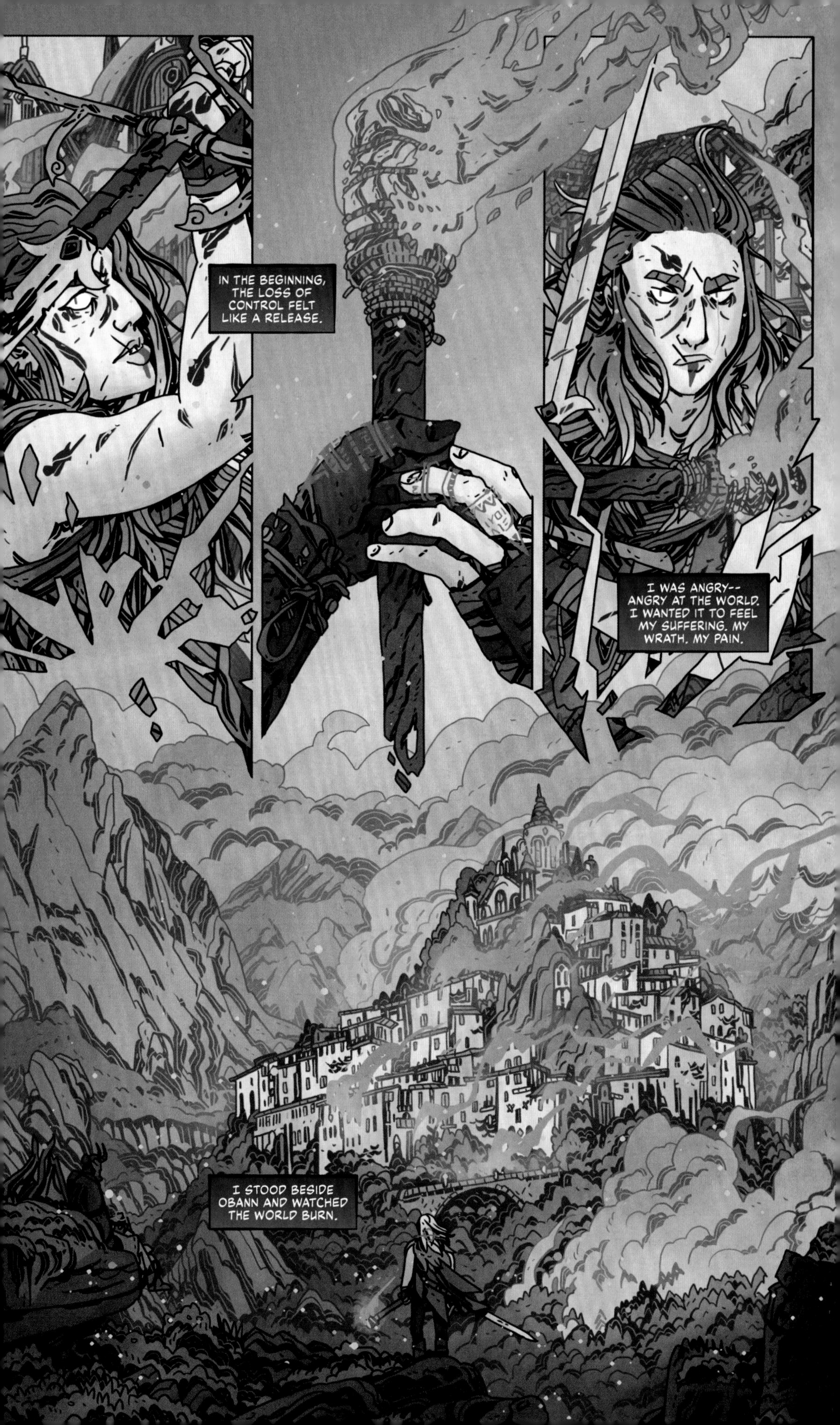
IN THE BEGINNING, THE LOSS OF CONTROL FELT LIKE A RELEASE.
I WAS ANGRY-- ANGRY AT THE WORLD. I WANTED IT TO FEEL MY SUFFERING. MY WRATH. MY PAIN.
I STOOD BESIDE OBANN AND WATCHED THE WORLD BURN.

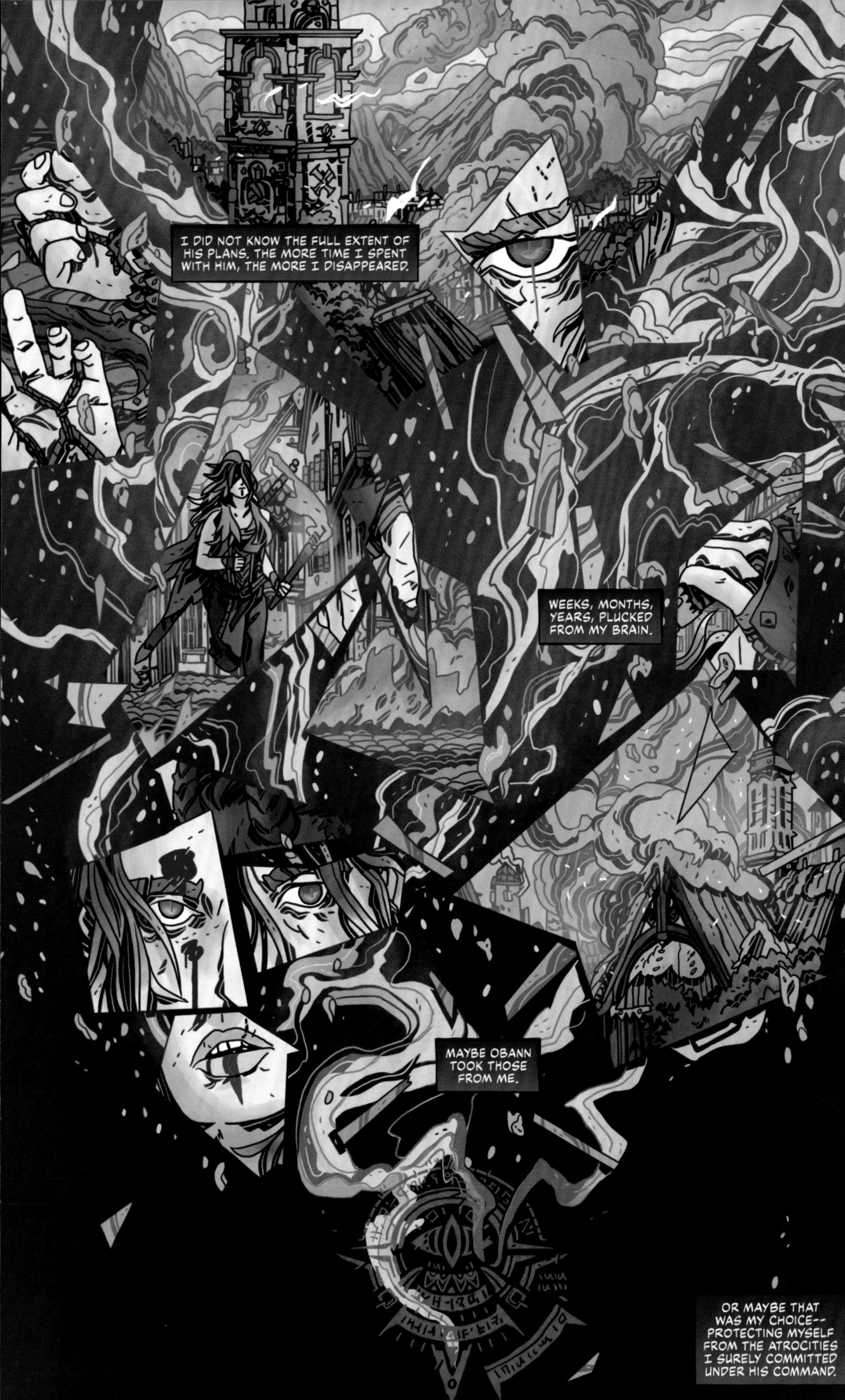
I DID NOT KNOW THE FULL EXTENT OF HIS PLANS. THE MORE TIME I SPENT WITH HIM, THE MORE I DISAPPEARED.
WEEKS, MONTHS, YEARS, PLUCKED FROM MY BRAIN.
MAYBE OBANN TOOK THOSE FROM ME.
OR MAYBE THAT WAS MY CHOICE--PROTECTING MYSELF FROM THE ATROCITIES I SURELY COMMITTED UNDER HIS COMMAND.

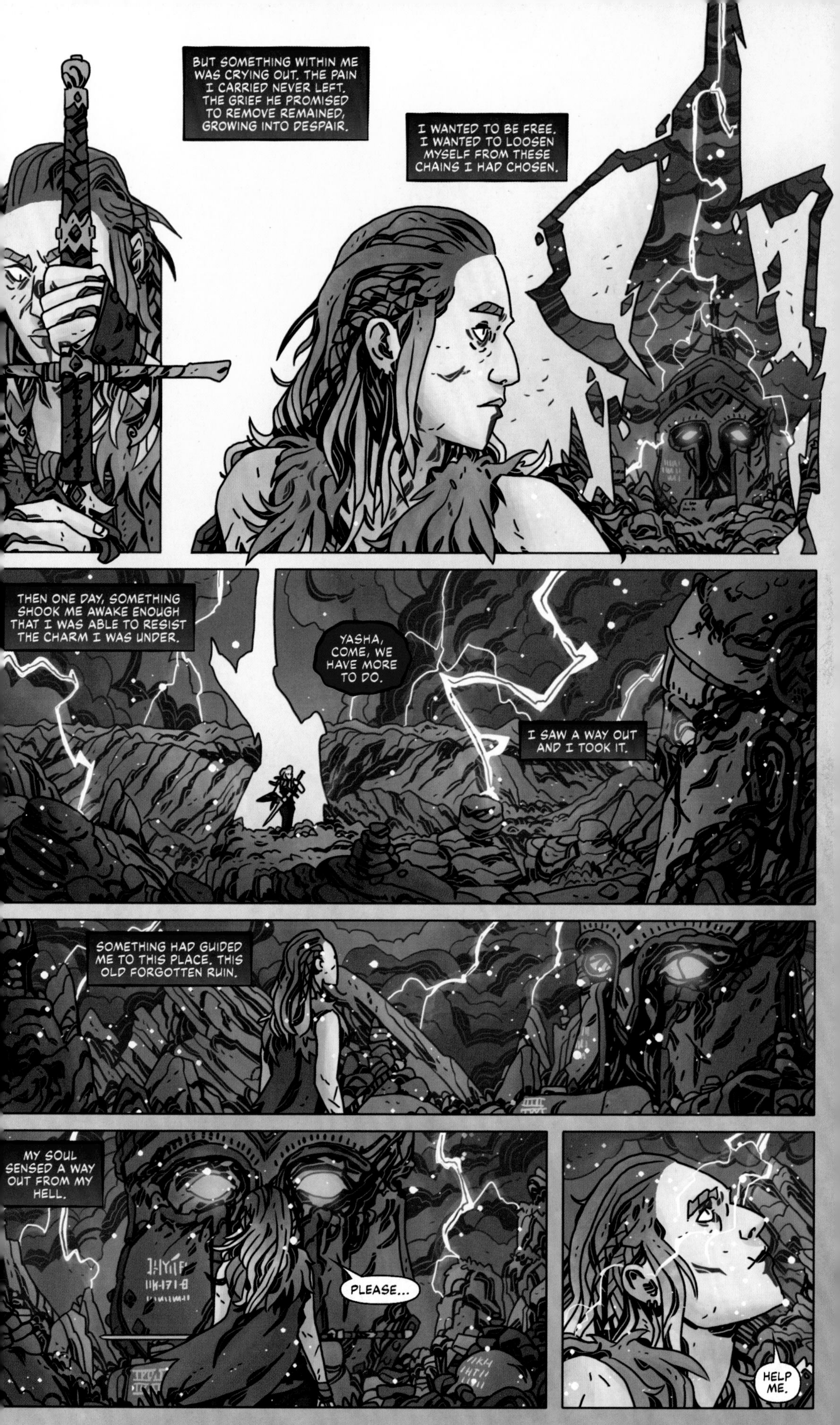
BUT SOMETHING WITHIN ME WAS CRYING OUT. THE PAIN I CARRIED NEVER LEFT. THE GRIEF HE PROMISED TO REMOVE REMAINED, GROWING INTO DESPAIR.
I WANTED TO BE FREE. I WANTED TO LOOSEN MYSELF FROM THESE CHAINS I HAD CHOSEN.
THEN ONE DAY, SOMETHING SHOOK ME AWAKE ENOUGH THAT I WAS ABLE TO RESIST THE CHARM I WAS UNDER.
YASHA, COME, WE HAVE MORE TO DO.
I SAW A WAY OUT AND I TOOK IT.
SOMETHING HAD GUIDED ME TO THIS PLACE. THIS OLD FORGOTTEN RUIN.
MY SOUL SENSED A WAY OUT FROM MY HELL.
PLEASE...
HELP ME.

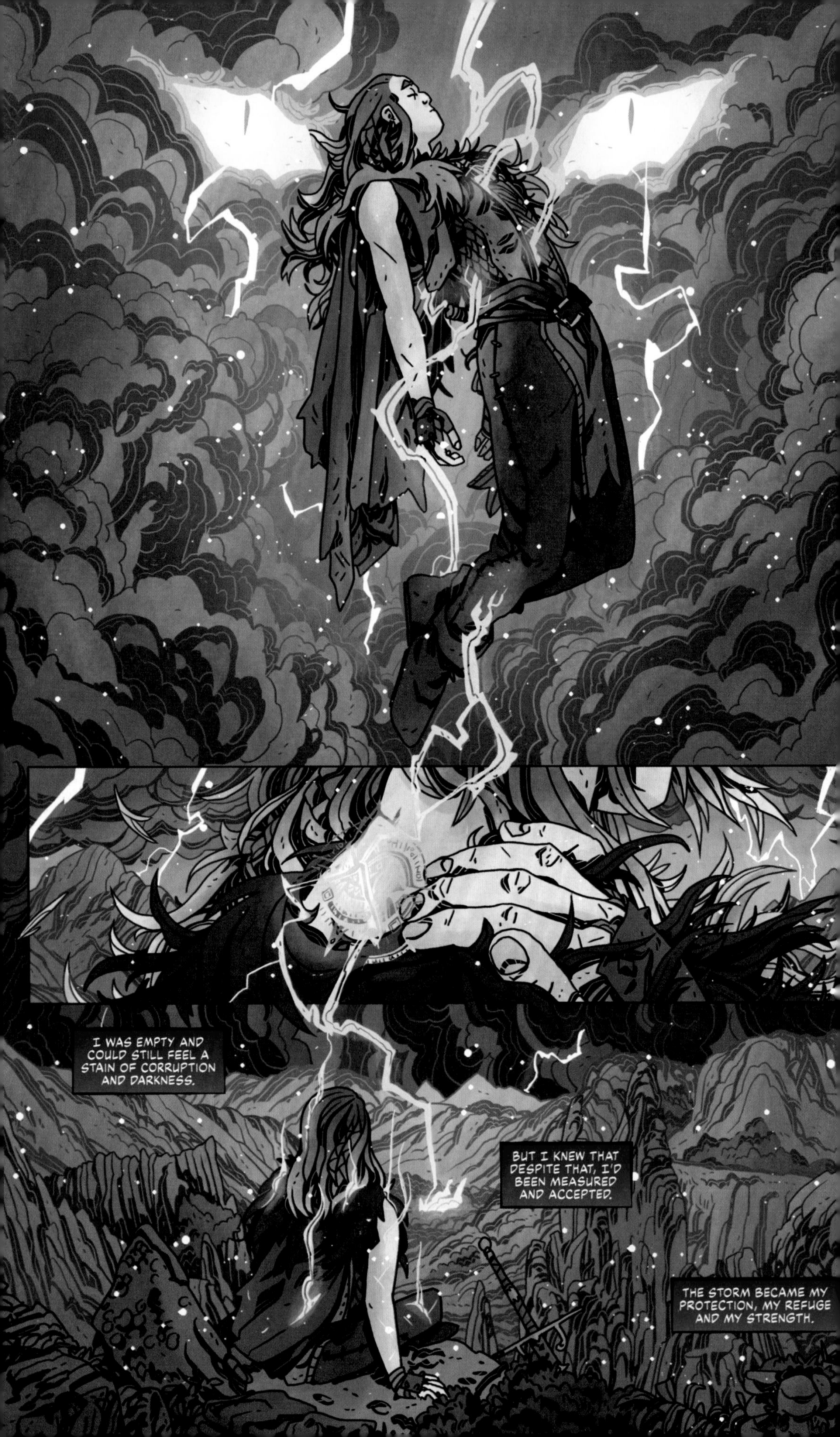
I WAS EMPTY AND COULD STILL FEEL A STAIN OF CORRUPTION AND DARKNESS.
BUT I KNEW THAT DESPITE THAT, I'D BEEN MEASURED AND ACCEPTED.
THE STORM BECAME MY PROTECTION, MY REFUGE AND MY STRENGTH.

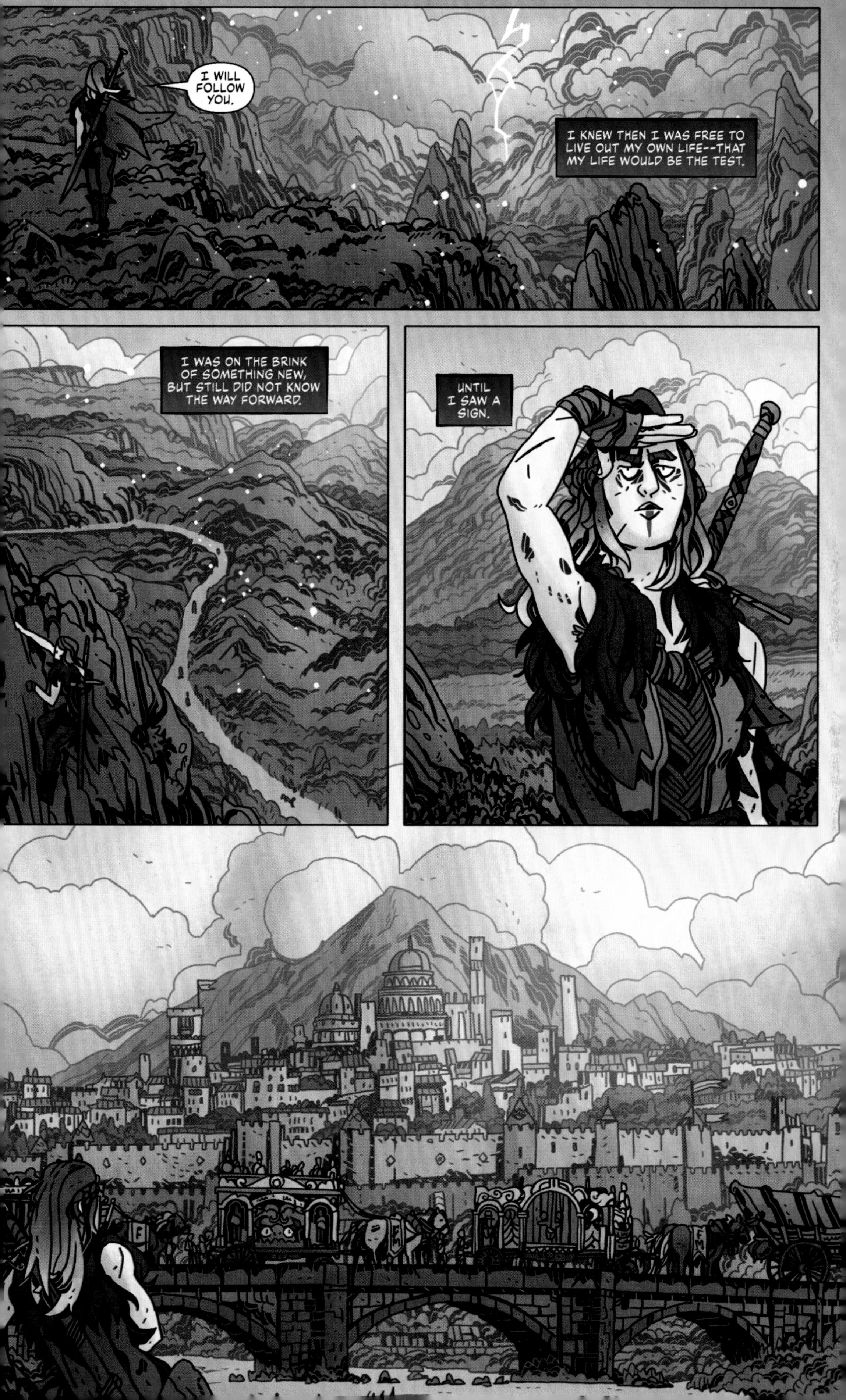
I WILL FOLLOW YOU.
I KNEW THEN I WAS FREE TO LIVE OUT MY OWN LIFE--THAT MY LIFE WOULD BE THE TEST.
I WAS ON THE BRINK OF SOMETHING NEW, BUT STILL DID NOT KNOW THE WAY FORWARD.
UNTIL I SAW A SIGN.

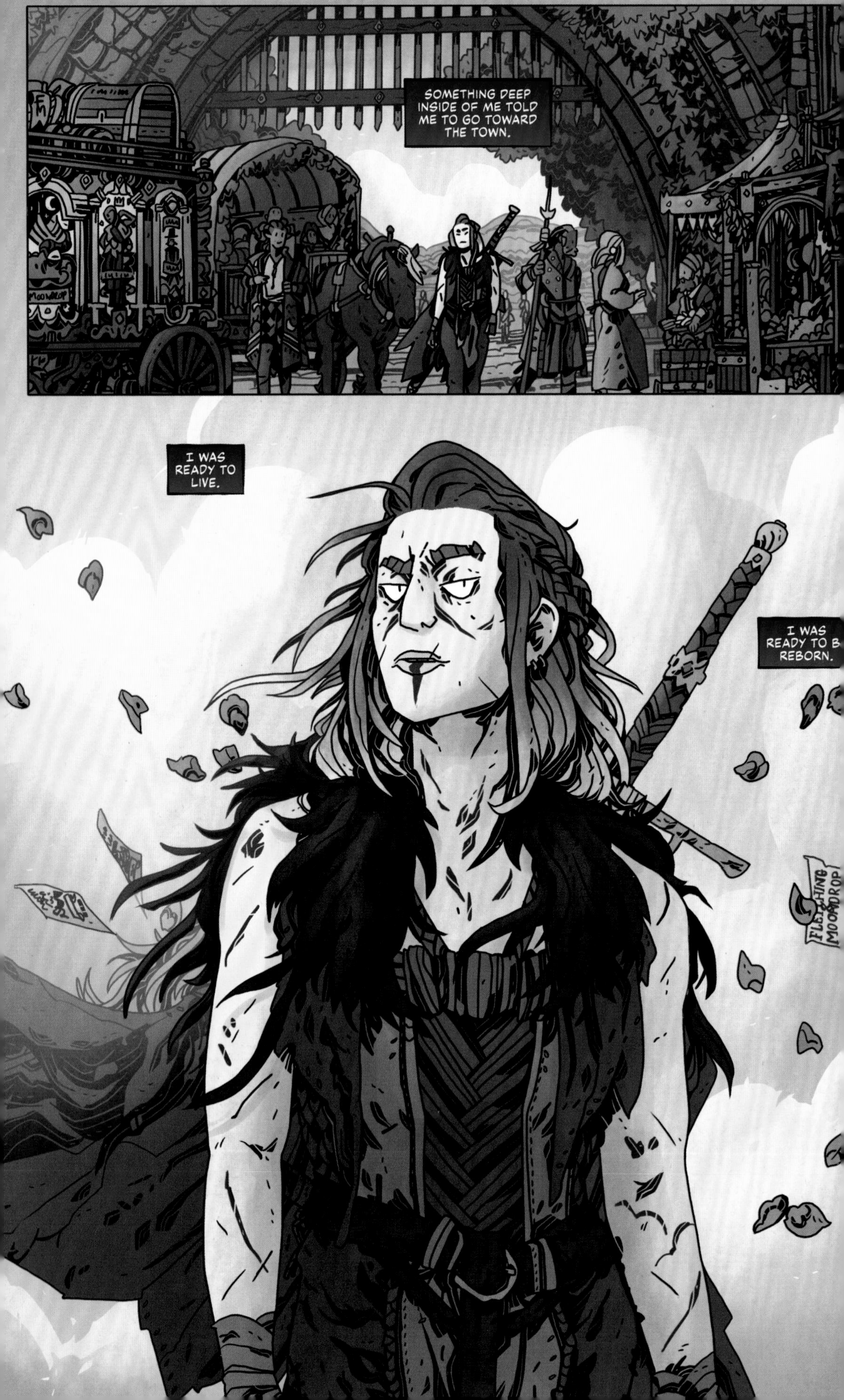
SOMETHING DEEP INSIDE OF ME TOLD ME TO GO TOWARD THE TOWN.
I WAS READY TO LIVE.
I WAS READY TO B REBORN.

Yasha's Sketchbook

ILLUSTRATIONS BY William Kirkby AND Diana Sousa ◆ COMMENTARY BY Rachel Roberts

CRITICAL ROLE
THE
MIGHTY·NEIN
ORIGINS
YASHA

CRITICAL ROLE
THE
MIGHTY·NEIN
ORIGINS
YASHA

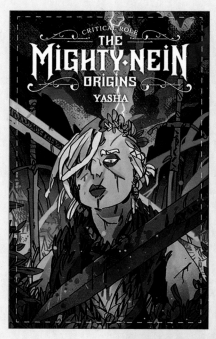

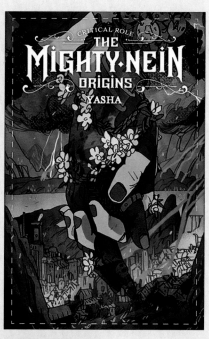

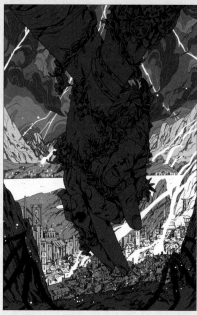

Will's cover sketches (*top*) are a feast for the eyes. While it's typical to feature the titular character on the cover, we couldn't pass up the imagery of Yasha and Zuala holding hands. The final line art (*bottom*) is beautiful in black and white.

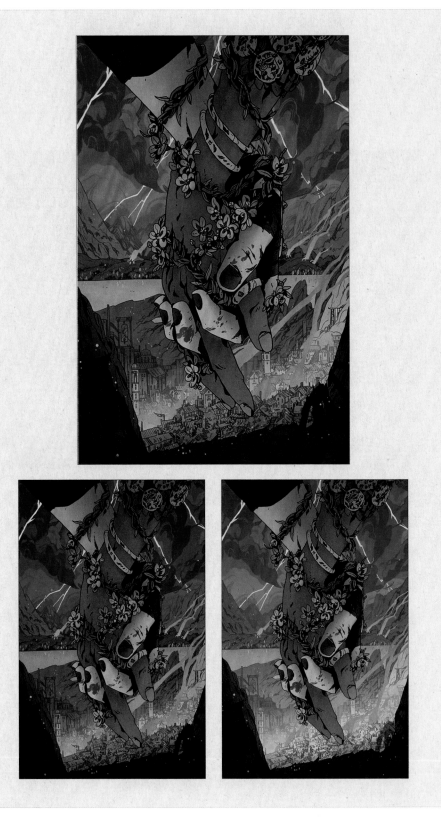

Colorist Diana Sousa submitted three color variations for the Critical Role team to choose from. The cooler options are beautiful, but the dark magenta of the final cover creates a strong contrast, making the characters' hands pop.

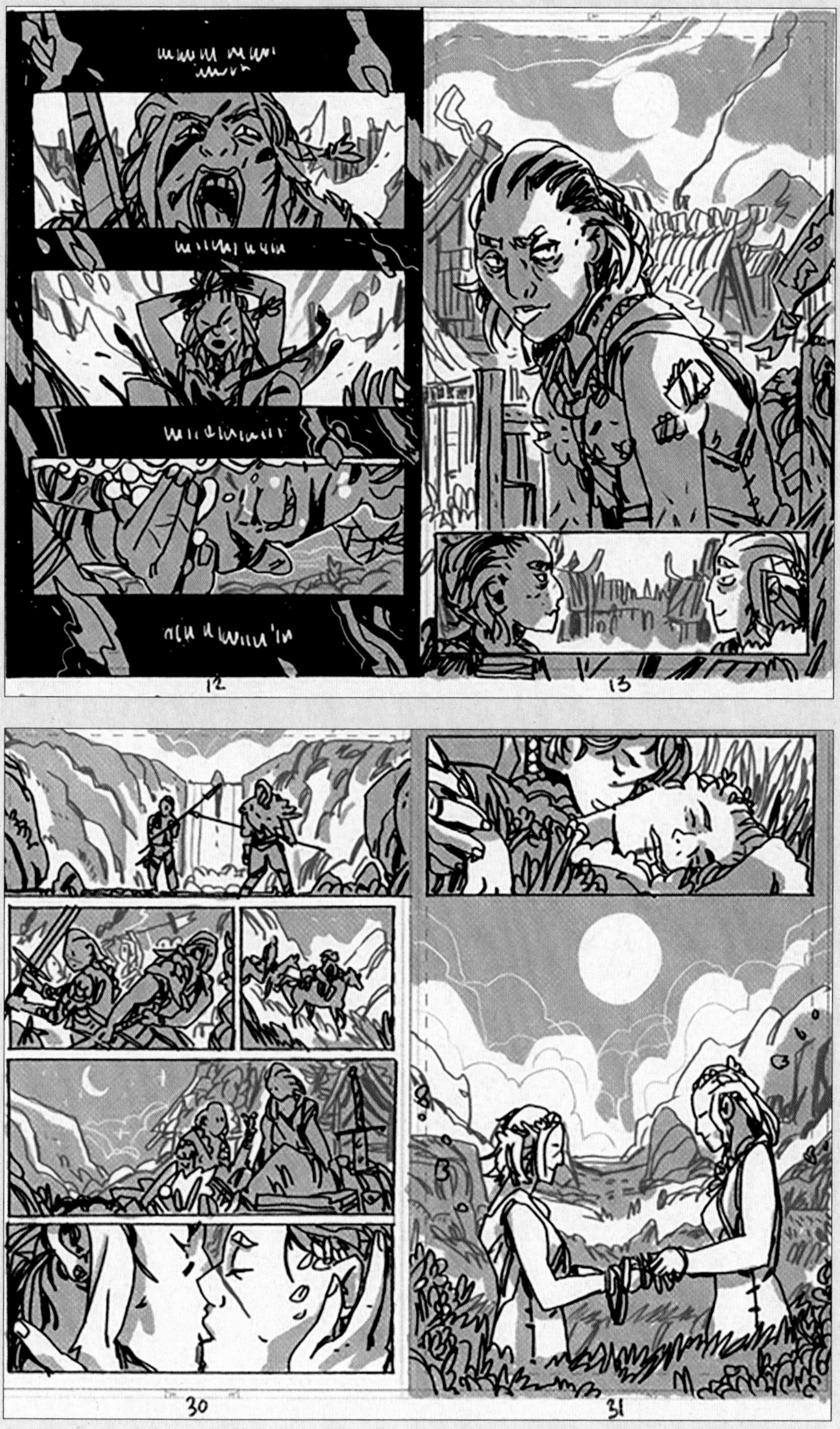
12
13
30
31

Will's initial layouts were detailed and strong. The additional turquoise shading helped all of the sequences and action read clearly, and we all felt as emotional reading the layouts as we did the script, and later, the final pages.

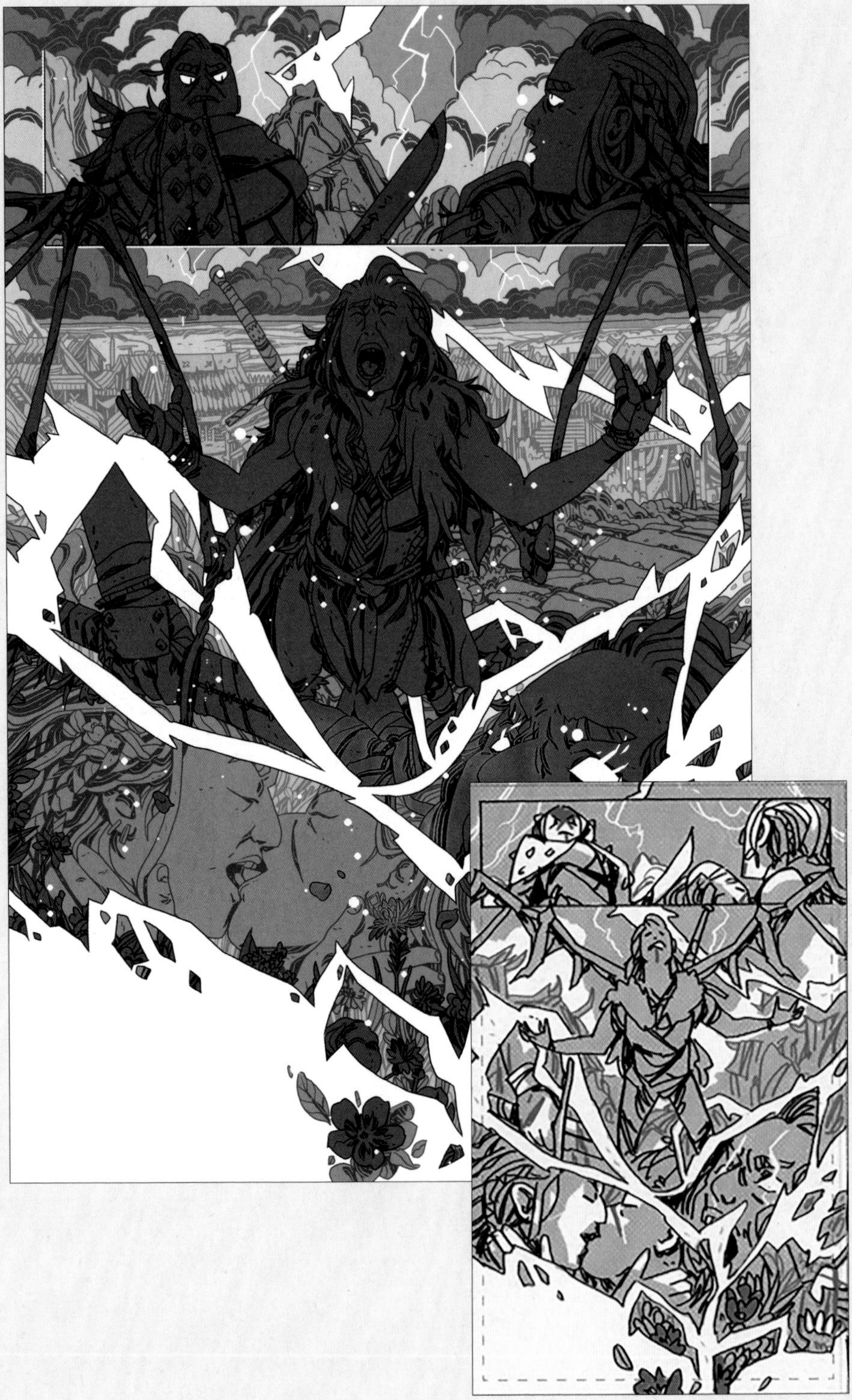

Comparing the layouts to the final pages shows off Will's incredible drafting skills. There weren't many changes between these two stages; the most notable changes were simply additional (and numerous) details.